SELF-ESTEEM: LOVING YOURSELF AT EVERY AGE

SELF-ESTEEM

Loving Yourself at Every Age

Jerry Aldridge

DOXA BOOKS
Birmingham, Alabama

Library of Congress Cataloging-in-Publication Data

Aldridge, Jerry.
    Self-esteem: loving yourself at every age / Jerry Aldridge.
    Includes bibliographical references and index.
    ISBN 0-9637034-0-4
    1. Self-esteem. 2. Developmental psychology. I. Title.
  BF697.5.S46A43   1993   93-11765
  155.2—dc20   CIP

Doxa Books
5316 Meadow Brook Road
Birmingham, Alabama 35242
10 9 8 7 6 5 4 3 2

Dedication

CONTENTS

Preface   13

How to Use This Book to Improve Your Own
Self-esteem and That of Others   15

Chapter 1   *Describing Self-esteem*   19
                What Is Self-esteem?   19
                    Self-esteem is developmental   21
                    Self-esteem is spiral   21
                    Self-esteem is a mirror   22
                    Self-esteem is both general and
                    specific   23
                    Self-esteem has many components   24
                    Self-esteem is difficult to measure   25
                What Is Required for High Self-esteem?   27
                    A sense of belonging   27
                    A feeling of individuality   29
                    The ability to choose   31
                    The presence of good models   32
                Where Do We Get Our Self-esteem?   33
                    The influence of others   33

The influence of institutions   34
The influence of personalities   35
The influence of experiences   35
The influence of history   36
The impact of environments and social
    class   37
The influence of the culture   37
The influence of our decisions   38

Chapter 2   **Developing Self-esteem in Infants
and Toddlers**   39

The Development of Bonding and
    Attachment   39
Acceptance of the Child's Temperament   42
The Child's Development of Trust and
    Autonomy   44
The Importance of the Parents'
    Self-esteem   45
Understanding Stranger Anxiety and
    Separation Anxiety   46
The Child's Mastery of Developmental
    Tasks   47
Dance of Synchronicity   48
Some More Practical Concrete
    Suggestions   49
Other Resources   50

Chapter 3   **Developing Self-esteem in Early
Childhood**   52

Suggestions to Build Self-esteem
    Through Play   61

Some More Practical Concrete
    Suggestions   62
Other Resources   63

Chapter 4   ***Developing Self-esteem in Middle***
                  Childhood   64

The Impact of Schooling   64
The Importance of the Parent
and School Partnership   65
The Effects of Stress on Self-esteem   66
    The child's personality   67
    The child's family   67
    Learning experiences   67
    The number of stressors   67
    Compensatory experiences   68
The Continuing Development of
    Individuality   68
    Types of intelligences   68
    Learning styles   69
    Personality traits   69
Some More Practical Concrete
    Suggestions   71
Other Resources   72

Chapter 5   ***Developing Self-esteem in***
                  Preadolescence   74

The Family and Self-esteem   75
The School   76
The Peer Group   76
Emerging Themes   78
    The cry of self-hatred   78
    The cry of psychological orphans   79

Some More Practical Concrete
   Suggestions   79
Other Resources   81

Chapter 6   ***Developing Self-esteem in Adolescence***   82
How Adolescents Describe Themselves   82
Parents and Teenagers' Self-esteem   83
   Social class and teenagers' self-esteem   84
   Physical appearance and teenagers'
   self-esteem   84
   Thinking abilities and teenagers'
   self-esteem   84
The Importance of Self-esteem   85
   Feelings of self-worth and adjustment   85
   Self-esteem and vocational choice   86
   Self-esteem and juvenile delinquency   87
Some More Practical Concrete
   Suggestions   87
Further Suggestions for Adolescents to
   Improve Their own Self-esteem   89
Other Resources   90

Chapter 7   ***Developing Self-esteem in Early
Adulthood***   91

Self-esteem and Love   91
Self-esteem and Work   93
   Having a well-rounded life   94
   Choosing a career you care about   94
   Working hard but not being a
   perfectionist   94
   The willingness to take risks   95
   Estimating your own abilities   95
   Competing with yourself   95

Going over or rehearsing difficult tasks 96
Some More Practical Concrete
   Suggestions   96
Other Resources   97

Chapter 8   ***Developing Self-esteem in Middle***
    Adulthood   98

The Need for a Balanced Life   98
Midlife Crisis and Self-worth   103
   Physical attractiveness   104
   Career adjustment in midlife   105
   Family issues in midlife   106
Dealing with the Dark Side of Life   107
The Search for Purpose   110
A New Look at the Mirror of
   Self-esteem   111
Some More Practical Concrete
   Suggestions   112
Other Resources   113

Chapter 9   ***Developing Self-esteem in Later***
    Adulthood   115

Some More Practical Concrete Suggestions
   for Developing and Maintaining Self-
   esteem in Late Adulthood   120
   What the elderly can do for
   themselves   121
   How you can help the elderly enhance
   their self-esteem   122
Other Resources   123

Chapter 10   ***Self-esteem and the Disabled***   125

Esteem Needs of Families Who Have
    Disabled Children   125
Self-esteem Needs of the Disabled   127
Five Self-esteem Rules for the Disabled
    and/or Their Families   128
Other Resources   131

Chapter 11 **Self-esteem and the Group**   132

Suggestions for Building Your Cultural
    and National Self-esteem   134
Self-esteem and Cultural Diversity   135
Suggestions for Building Your
    Subcultural Self-esteem   136
Self-esteem and Women   136
Suggestions for Women in Building
    Their Own Self-esteem   137
Other Resources   137

Chapter 12 **Conclusions—Decisions for
Self-esteem**   139

Seven Decisions to Make   139
The Map Maker   141

Index   145

PREFACE

Self-esteem is much like the weather. Everyone talks about it but very few do anything about it. There have been volumes written about self-esteem and how to improve it. The reader might ask, "Why do we need another book on self-esteem? Just how is this book different?"

In answer to these two questions, the following features make this book unique:

1. Self-esteem is described across the lifespan. This includes the period of preadolescence (ages nine to thirteen) which is a distinct period in life rarely addressed. Suggestions are made on how to build self-esteem for each developmental phase of life.

2. Self-esteem is explained as both general and specific. People have a general feeling of self-worth but also self-esteems in many specific areas.

3. Self-esteem is considered to be a spiral. Each of us has individual themes which come around again and again. Our reactions to these themes influence our self-regard.

4. Self-esteem is also described as group or cultural. We each have individual self-esteems, and we participate in the collective, cultural or national self-esteem.

5. Self-esteem is discussed with regard to the dark side of life.

What the dark side has to do with self-worth is explained.

6. Special situations are also considered. The differently abled, the culturally diverse, and women are presented in terms of their needs for self-esteem.

This book tells you what to do to improve self-worth throughout life—your own life and the lives of those around you. Unfortunately, I cannot tell you *how* to do it for this is always individual. The how-to's are as diverse as the number of people on the planet. However, when we discover what is needed for self-esteem it is exciting to see our own uniqueness and individual ways we can use for building it.

A special thanks to Rozilah (Rozz) bin Embi for his invaluable help with the layout, formatting, and the editing of the text. His commitment and untiring work expedited the overall time-line of the book.

I would also like to thank the following people for their contributions to the text. I am indebted to Dr. Kay Knowlton of Counseling Associates, Dr. Nancy Qualls-Corbett, a psychologist and Jungian analyst, and Dr. Gene Qualls, a pediatrician and psychotherapist for their encouragement. Other people who influenced this manuscript include Dr. Marion Nissen of Livingston University, Dr. Tommy Russell and Dr. Carol Schlichter of the University of Alabama, Dr. Joellen Harris of Anderson College, Drs. Anne Leen, Larry Kessler, Nelly Hecker, Hazel Harris, Bill Teska, Sallie Grant, and A. Bing Somers, all of Furman University. Also, Drs. Jean Ann Box and Janice Teale of Samford University, Dr. Robert J. Canady of Marymount University, Dr. Shirley Raines of the University of South Florida, Drs. David Sexton and Randall Scott of the University of New Orleans, Dr. Judy W. Wood of Virginia Commonwealth University, Dr. J. Richard Gentry of Western Carolina University, and Mr. Richard Cecil of University of Alabama. All of these individuals were helpful in the formation of this book.

A special word of thanks goes to my former doctoral students, Drs. Patricia Kuby and Debi Strevy for their help with references.

I am especially grateful to my friends whose support, suggestions, and encouragement were helpful. These include Todd Fatzinger, Judy White, Susan Avery, Bernice Farris, Linda Steele, Keith Miller, Larry Salvati, and Kay Emfinger.

Finally, I would like to dedicate this book to my family. I have been truly blessed with two wonderful parents, Rev. J. Titus Aldridge and Winnie Sims Aldridge, whose acceptance and encouragement have always been my strong sense of inspiration. I have also had the support of other family members who include Gay Trawick, Jessica and Bruce Capp, and C. Michael Baker. I wish to honor the following family and friends who have died: Dolly Sims, Willow Dean Martin, Christopher L. Farris, Rodger C. Sanders, Gladys Baker, Verla Burroughs, and Larry Brunson. Also, a warm tribute to Embi bin Long of Malacca, Malaysia—a great man departed leaving nine children of whom two I know and enjoy.

HOW TO USE THIS BOOK TO IMPROVE YOUR OWN SELF-ESTEEM AND THAT OF OTHERS

Have you ever been on a trip without a roadmap? Low self-esteem is often a journey through the wilderness without a map. *Self-esteem: Loving Yourself at Every Age* is a guide for what you need on your self-esteem journey throughout life.

Self-esteem was written with everyone in mind from the newborn to the one hundred two year old. It is designed to help you understand self-esteem from womb to tomb.

There are many books written on self-esteem, but I have not seen any like this one which takes a lifespan approach. I believe that it is important for you to know how self-esteem develops in the early years so that you can now capitalize on past efforts at self-esteem. This will help you remedy the prior incidents which might have gotten in the way of your present self-esteem. It is also important for you to know how self-esteem can be promoted at ages beyond yours so you can make adequate preparations now for the future.

This book is full of practical suggestions for helping everyone at every stage of life improve on their self-esteem. Find out in chapter one what self-esteem is, where we get it, and what is necessary to improve it.

Self-esteem needs change on your journey as you move from a small child to a senior adult. Chapters two through nine are written about specific ages and times when these self-esteem needs change. You can use these chapters to help you select the equipment necessary for the ever changing journey on the road to higher self-esteem.

Try out the suggestions of the book on yourself first. You will be a better tour guide toward positive self-regard if you have embarked on the journey yourself. It's hard to help fellow travelers if you have not journeyed this way before.

Then you can use this book to accept and encourage others you meet along the path. Not everyone's travels will take them where you are, but as you meet others on the road you can help them through their life's expedition by considering their age and needs described in the many chapters which follow.

To help yourself and others you will want to consider the many examples and suggestions provided. *Self-esteem: Loving Yourself at Every Age* is full of suggestions throughout each chapter. At the end of most chapters there is also a section entitled "Some More Practical Concrete Suggestions." How is your situation and your family's similar or different from the people described in the following pages? Can you come up with your own personal examples about self-esteem from the pages of your own life? Can you think of ways to apply the ideas to your own life and those whose lives you touch?

Most of all, use this book to have fun and enjoy yourself. Trying to put the puzzle pieces of your life together is often challenging and frustrating, but with a little help it can be down right fun.

Some people say life is rough and then you die. I say life is for learning and the most difficult person to learn about is yourself. I hope you enjoy your journey into your own self-worth as much as I have into mine. It has not always been easy for me nor has it been continually fun, but I have learned a lot about me, and I hope you will learn much about you.

CHAPTER ONE

DESCRIBING SELF-ESTEEM

The opportunity to find out who we are always comes to us. Every life situation brings with it the question, "Who are we?" With it comes the chance for an authentic answer. At the same time, family background, upbringing, religion, culture, and other people's desires bring the temptation to be something other than ourselves. When we choose to be anything other than who we are, we develop anxieties and are plagued with fears. Why do most of us choose to be something other than who we are? Could it be the fear of finding out who we really are? This entire book is devoted to helping us value who we are and to building self-esteem throughout life.

In this first chapter we will consider three important questions. These are (1) *What is self-esteem?* (2) *What is required for high self-esteem?* and (3) *Where do we get our self-esteem?*

WHAT IS SELF-ESTEEM?

Just what is self-esteem? In order to answer this question, self-esteem must be contrasted with three other terms which have been used interchangeably with it. These include self-image, self-concept, and self-confidence.

Self-image refers to how we picture ourselves. It is the image of

19

how we look in terms of our physical selves. Self-image influences our self-esteem, but it is not the same thing. Self-image is particularly important to teenagers, and the image of what we look like as adults sometimes stems back to adolescence. I tend to have a self-image of someone thin. When I was in high school I was six feet tall and weighed 137 pounds. In graduate school when I reached 220 pounds and people referred to me as fat, I still had that image of my 137 pound high school self. My physical appearance had changed but not my self-image.

Self-concept is the thinking part of the self. It is what we think we are. People can think of themselves as many different things. We can think of ourselves as pianists, parents, football players, grandparents, lawyers, physicians, maids, and many other categories and jobs.

Self-confidence is what we believe we can do. When we approach a new situation, it often takes courage and self-confidence to attempt this and know that we will succeed. Self-confidence, though, is not self-esteem. There are many people who believe they can do many things. They will attempt new things but do not necessarily feel good about themselves.

So, *what is self-esteem?* It is the feeling part of the self. A person's self-concept might be that of a mother. The woman sees herself as the mother of three young children, but how does she feel about herself as a mother? Does she feel competent? Unworthy? Excited? Overwhelmed?

Self-esteem is the feeling of self-worth and *high self-regard.* The terms *self-esteem, self-worth,* and *self-regard* will be used as synonyms throughout this book. However, s*elf-image, self-concept,* and *self-confidence* will be used to mean something else.

Self-esteem is multidimensional and can be viewed in many different ways. It is developmental and changes over time. It is like a spiral and a mirror and is both general and specific. Self-esteem has many parts which include behaviors, feelings, evaluations, and motivations. Because of its many facets, self-esteem is very difficult to measure.

Self-esteem Is Developmental

Self-esteem is developmental which means it changes over time. Our general feelings about ourselves may not change over time. Some people have low self-regard throughout their entire lives while others have fairly high self-worth over time. Self-esteem does not have to be constant, it can change.

What does change about self-esteem? One thing that does change over time is what influences self-esteem. Very early in life we are dependent upon our parents for self-worth. When we enter school teachers contribute to self-regard. Over time, peers have a stronger influence. By the time we are adults the circle of influence has widened to include intimate relationships and our jobs. By midlife a developing inner life can contribute much and by old age everything from grandchildren to hobbies and leisure activities can affect us. The people and situations which influence self-esteem change over time. This is why self-esteem is developmental.

Self-esteem Is Spiral

Many psychologists see development as moving in a straight line while others see changes over time in steps or stages. Self-esteem, though, is neither linear nor step-like. It is an ever deepening and widening spiral. Certain themes of self-esteem repeat themselves over and over. This repeating of themes is always individual. Every person has themes which come around again. Life has a wonderful way of bringing a theme back to us until we learn to love ourselves in the theme's context.

The following is an example of a spiraling theme of self-esteem as it is played out in one person's life. Rachel is a forty-two-year-old woman who feels good as a daughter, as a lawyer, and as a friend. She has high self-esteem in all of these specific areas. However, Rachel has low self-worth within a marriage. She feels ugly, sexually unattractive, and would do anything to have an intimate relationship with the opposite sex, including denying her own individuality. She is consumed with wanting a relationship, but her low self-esteem (in this area) prevents this from happening.

Rachel's first marriage was a disaster. Her husband did not work, and he physically and verbally abused her. Rachel resented this but felt this marriage was the best she could do. The marriage ended in divorce.

Rachel's relationship theme emerged again but at a deeper level. It spiraled around again. Her second marriage was not very satisfying, but it seemed better than the first. Her second husband had a job. He was not physically abusive, but he was verbally cruel. Again, she felt this was the best she could do because of her low self-regard. She tried desperately to please her husband. She used all the money she made as a lawyer to support the household while her husband spent his money on fancy cars, boats, and other women. Rachel did everything she could to think of to make the marriage work. She neglected most of her own needs to try to make her husband love her.

One Saturday when her husband was on his boat with another woman, Rachel found out about it. She called a friend and said, almost without thinking, "I'm doing all I can in my marriage to prove I am unlovable." Indeed she was. The second marriage also ended in divorce. **Did Rachel learn anything this time about love relationships and self-esteem and what she is really trying to prove?** Hopefully Rachel is paying attention. This relationship and self-esteem theme will spiral around again at a deeper level. Rachel feels good about herself as a daughter, lawyer, and friend, and these worlds reflect how she feels about them. Her husbands also mirrored the way she felt about herself in a marriage relationship—unlovable.

Self-esteem Is a Mirror

From the example of Rachel we can see that self-esteem is not only a spiral but also a mirror. The looking glass theory of self-esteem is by no means new. The famous social psychologist George Mead wrote about this in his 1934 book entitled *Mind, Self, and*

Society. Self-esteem acts as a mirror of how others see us, and it shows how we feel about ourselves. It's hard to tell the difference between the two. Do we feel unlovable because others believe we are, or do others see us as unlovable because we act that way? When we have low self-regard the mirror reflects a vicious cycle. Close attention to what is happening is necessary in order to break this reflection and form a new one. Like Rachel, most of us feel good about some aspects of ourselves and bad about others. We have specific areas in which we feel worthy and others where we do not like who we are.

Self-esteem Is Both General and Specific

Self-esteem can be seen as general and specific; both can be found in every person. There is a global, general, or overall self-regard. Then there are specific self-esteems. We may feel generally good about ourselves (general self-esteem) but really bad about our worth in a specific area (specific self-esteem).

Certain points can be made about general and specific self-esteem. First, general self-esteem is not the sum of all our specific self-esteems. Our total self-esteem is partially due to the importance we give some of our specific self-esteems.

Second, everybody decides how much importance to give their specific self-esteems. Rachel places a lot of weight on a good opposite-sex relationship and very little in other areas. Therefore, her general self-esteem is very low. Another person similar to Rachel and Rachel's history might weight work very high for her self-esteem and marriage extremely low. This person would conceivably have higher general self-regard. It is partly a matter of how much weight we give our specific self-esteems.

Third, changes in specific self-esteem cannot always be expected to change general self-esteem. A good example would be the idea of helping low achievers in school do better in order to improve their general self-esteem. This may or may not be true depending on how each individual weights school achievement in terms of their general self-worth. If a person does not care at all for school, improving school performance isn't likely to influence overall self-esteem.

Fourth, there are many specific self-esteems; there are many different lives we live. Just how many specific areas of self-esteem are there? The answer is based on each individual person. British author Jeanette Winterson believes that we are all multiple and not single beings. We are many people in one, holding hands like cut-out paper dolls.

When I was in high school and college I was the Drum Major of the band. I saw myself as a Drum Major *(self-concept)* and *felt* very good about myself as a Drum Major *(self-esteem)*. That specific area of self-esteem was very different from everyone else in the school (since I was the only Drum Major at the time).

The specific areas of self-esteem change over time. I am no longer a Drum Major. I no longer see myself as a Drum Major and so what was once a specific area of my self-esteem is no longer. Everyone's specific self-esteems are unique and they change over time.

Self-esteem Has Many Components

Self-esteem is made up of many parts. These include behavioral, attitudinal, evaluative, and motivational aspects. While self-esteem is how we feel about ourselves, what makes up these feelings (both general and specific) is dependent on these four parts.

Self-regard involves *behavior*. Two four-year-old boys perform different behaviors. One plays with a doll and the other with a football. One, unfortunately, is scolded while the other is praised. Their behaviors influence others who in turn influence them. How people respond to behavior strongly affects self-worth.

Self-esteem has an *attitudinal* component. The boy who is scolded for playing with dolls gets the feeling that something is wrong with his behavior. He, as a consequence may begin to feel that something is wrong with him. The boy who is praised for playing with a football develops the idea that he is OK. Of course the attitudes we develop about ourselves are not usually based on single events but multiple happenings and the reflections made by ourselves and others.

Our attitudes are very important to our self-regard. They are often difficult to separate from *evaluations* since attitudes usually imply some type of evaluation, some likes or dislikes. The normal developmental progression of how we evaluate ourselves is a move from the importance of outer opinions to inner ones. Unfortunately, many never make this move from ideas about themselves based on others' opinions. At first, though, outer evaluations are where we learn to view ourselves and establish our feelings about ourselves. As adults, we are responsible for how we view ourselves.

The *motivational* aspects of self-worth are often unconscious. As we grow older we are motivated to maintain the feelings we have developed. We seek to maintain and confirm our true feelings about ourselves—no matter how high; no matter how low. Rachel has been trying to prove she is unlovable in a relationship and confirm her low self-esteem. The motivational aspects of self-esteem are highly resistant to change unless we become conscious of these motivations (of what we are really trying to prove).

Self-esteem Is Difficult to Measure

Self-esteem is difficult if not impossible to measure. Many experimental psychologists do not believe self-esteem should be a topic of investigation because it is not directly observable or measurable. The more important an issue is in life the more difficult it will be to understand or measure it. How do we measure love? A poem? God? Just because self-worth is difficult to describe or evaluate does not make it unworthy of our efforts to explore it—quite the contrary.

Self-esteem tests are sometimes poor tests of self-esteem. Why is this? There are many reasons, such as the fact that a person can lie. Also the exams are often poorly constructed. For example, many self-esteem tests provide a general score of self-esteem based on the cumulative scores of specific areas. These measures have been criticized because general self-esteem is not the sum of specific self-esteems. Remember, what is important is how we individually weight each specific area.

Self-esteem is also difficult to test at certain ages. How can we evaluate an infant's self-esteem? Do teenagers tell the truth about their self-worth? Every age of the lifespan has its own problems with measurement.

Self-esteem is also difficult to evaluate because of **where** tests are given. Paper and pencil tests or oral questions given in a room by a stranger can never tell as much about an individual's self-esteem as interactions with people on a daily basis.

What we measure is always limited. Since every person's specific self-esteem areas are different and weighted unequally, how could we possibly think of all the combinations and considerations to accurately measure self-worth development?

Finally, **who** does the evaluating makes a big difference, especially when using casual observations. Inferences are often made which are inaccurate. For example, a kindergarten child was found to always draw with black, brown, and grey crayons. His teacher thought he must be depressed or expressing low self-esteem. A closer look revealed he was the last person on his row to receive the one crayon box which everyone used during drawing time. The only colors left when he got the box were brown, black, and grey!

Self-esteem is complex and elusive. It is spiral and reflective, both general and specific. It has behavioral, attitudinal, evaluative, and motivational aspects. These components interact with each other to alter self-regard. All of this makes a person's self-esteem difficult to determine. However, it is vitally important. Self-worth is more important to school success and life adjustment than intelligence. Few things in life are more important than learning to love ourselves.

WHAT IS REQUIRED FOR HIGH SELF-ESTEEM?

There are four requirements for overall or general self-esteem. A sense of belonging, a feeling of individuality, the ability to choose, and the presence of good models are all necessary for healthy, positive self-regard in early development. Adults also base their self-esteem on such things as intimacy, a sense of purpose and meaning, and the feeling that good choices were made in the past. These adult issues are discussed in chapters seven through nine.

A Sense of Belonging

One of the major needs of life is to feel that we belong. Over time, where we get our sense of belonging changes. Very young children get their connectedness through the family and child care settings. As children reach kindergarten and the primary grades, their sense of belonging is widened to include school and their teachers. Children approaching middle school and high school usually develop a strong need to be a part of the peer group. Special clubs, cliques, or networks pervade high school life. High school is a time when we are often the most active in peer group activities—always looking for that group which will unconditionally accept us. In early adulthood our sense of belonging often shifts to a significant other as we establish intimacy in a relationship we sometimes hope will last a lifetime. Midlife is a time of transition and crises. Early in middle adulthood we may still be concerned with climbing the corporate ladder or getting needs met through our children, but ultimately the need for belonging shifts to a higher source—to finding that source which guides our lives. The sunset years are experienced as a connectedness or belonging with the past and the preparation for departing all relationships to which we belong.

*Three things impede our sense of belonging. These are what I call the deadly "c"s because they each begin with the letter "c." They are **comparison, competition,** and **conformity**.*

Comparison seems to be the American way of life. We are continually compared as a culture to the Japanese or the Europeans with the idea of catching up, getting ahead, or staying ahead. In business we are compared with our colleagues. We compare our children with one another and the neighbor's kids. *Comparisons* can only lead to externally oriented self-esteem which will ultimately fail.

In the myth of *Amor and Psyche* we see Psyche's sisters comparing themselves to her. Psyche is beautiful and innocent; they are homely like Cinderella's stepsisters. C. S. Lewis' novel *Till We Have Faces* is told from one of Psyche's sister's perspective. Oreul spends her entire life living through Psyche and lamenting the fact that she is not physically beautiful like Psyche. Yet Oreul has her own strengths. She is a loving, caring woman of strong character who has her own life to live and fulfill her own destiny. Because she no longer controls Psyche's life when Psyche grows up, Oreul feels she does not belong anywhere, even though she becomes the queen of her own country. When we compare ourselves with anyone else, we fall short of what we think we should be. We feel we don't belong. A sense of belonging is vital to self-worth, but it is no more important than bringing forth uniqueness.

Competition is the next deadly "c" to our sense of belonging. Competition is also pervasive in Western cultures. Most have heard the slogan, "Winning isn't everything. It's the only thing." What is particularly dangerous about competition and self-esteem is that it comes so early to our children. In the 1940s through the 1960s high competitiveness was reserved at least until junior high school. Today we have peewee football, beauty pageants for preschoolers, and other nonsense which throws children into competition before they have a chance to be a child and develop a strong ego so vital for self-regard. This problem is described in more detail in chapter three.

Competition heightens in adolescence and continues throughout life. As adults this *competition* is equally unfulfilling. It throws us into a world of "shoulds" to which we never seem to measure up. These shoulds are experienced through the *having, doing,* or *being* modes. We have to have a finer car than our neighbors. We have to do more than someone else to prove we are lovable, or we have to be something we are not to please someone else. We are competing with others for our own self-worth, and it doesn't seem enough— it never seems to work. Even when we feel it does, our efforts are in vain. It has been said that the only thing worse than failure (through *competition*) is success. If we are lucky enough to recognize this before life is over we have a chance of developing authentic self-esteem.

The third deterrent to our sense of belonging is *conformity*. At some time in our lives we all give up who we are in order to *conform* and be a part of the group. The problem with this is it is our persona or mask which belongs to the group, and we find who we really are is either unknown, not experienced, not valued or unauthentic. When we give up who we are to belong to the group we lose part of ourselves—a part which should be valued.

This *conformity* also starts very early in life. We use coloring books in which we have to stay in the lines, or we have to draw pictures or make projects like everyone else. In school, clubs, and religious groups we conform to a rigid set of beliefs in order to be accepted. In business we conform to beliefs and practices to which we do not agree in order to keep our jobs or climb the ladder of success. The price of this *conformity* is a lack of creativity, and the result is we become like everyone else. The truth is we are never allowed to become who we are for the sake of the group, and the irony is we can never truly feel a part of something unless our own uniqueness is also valued.

A Feeling of Individuality

Just as we need a sense of belonging, we also need to feel our own *individuality*—our uniqueness. Uniqueness is something we strive for even when we feel inferior. As the next chapter points out, we are all born with a unique temperament. Our personality traits and our strengths and weaknesses are part of this *individuality*.

In Western societies the concept of physical beauty is overstated in relation to our uniqueness. Commercials and the media present a particular body type which is often unachieveable. Looks are only one part of our individuality. If we are consumed with thoughts of looking good as the media suggest we do, then we miss finding out other things which make us special.

Individuality can be expressed through what we know, our talents, special skills, our cultural heritage, our hobbies, and what we do. A good example of someone with a sense of uniqueness is a developmentally delayed child named Jacqueline. Jacqueline was in a special education classroom when she transferred to another school. She was placed in a regular third grade class at her new school. Her new teacher asked Jacqueline to tell the class something about herself. Jacqueline had been studying marsupials (animals with pouches) at her previous school and had become very interested in learning about kangaroos. She was able to express her knowledge on the topic to her new classmates, and they were very impressed. Jacqueline's new teacher telephoned her former one to find out if the child had actually been in special education. Jacqueline had found something unique about herself which she was able to share.

Adolescence is a particularly vulnerable time for the feeling of *individuality*—a time when most teens want so much to be a part of the group. Adolescent misconduct is often a sign that the feeling of *individuality* is low. Children and adolescents may not know the reason for their bizarre behaviors, but it is often an indication that they are searching for what makes them special while at the same time trying to fit into that group to which they want to belong.

In early adulthood the search for *individuality* is often attempted through mate selection and career involvement. We seek to find our uniqueness through establishing relationships and making our contribution at work. By middle adulthood, however, we find that even if we are successful we are still lacking in our feeling of uniqueness. It is often at this time that we begin to seek spiritual answers in a quest for finding out who we are and why we are really here. During old age we still want to feel that we are worthy and attempt to cope with the choices we have made for uniqueness throughout life. Were our choices right for us? Did we bring forth what we were created to do or did we get our *individuality* from what others thought we should be? The sense of *individuality* is a constant source of self-esteem.

The Ability to Choose

The opportunity to make choices is important because it indicates that we have some power and control over certain aspects of our lives. The *ability to choose* develops over time. It begins in early childhood when we are given a chance to choose whether or not to wear the blue shirt or the green one to school. The power increases as we reach the elementary years and seek to choose our friends. By adolescence we make decisions about who we are. We have some choice in taking a spouse, choosing a career, deciding where we live, and how we spend our leisure time.

Power is associated with our *ability to choose*. The issue of power and self-worth is a two-edged sword. If our needs for power are respected when we are young then we can move on to other issues such as spiritual development. If, however, we experienced restricted opportunities to choose, then, our choices in adult life will often be for power rather than spiritual growth. We all know with our heads that there are certain things we have control over and certain things we do not. We may know this with our heads, but rarely do we experience this in our hearts. Many times adult life is spent trying to gain control over that which we cannot or should not have control. Running a business is one thing; running other people's lives is another. When we try to control other people's lives it is usually a sign that we are too afraid to look at ourselves. We sometimes make the choice of attending to anything other than painfully looking into our own psyches.

Choosing wisely involves legitimate suffering as opposed to neurotic suffering caused by unwise choices. If we are obese we learn with help from a specialist to wisely choose a diet and go through the real pain we find in reducing. If we choose to have our "stomach stapled" so we can eat what we want and still lose weight we may suffer more. As we age, we attend to our health and looks as legitimately as we can. If we are consumed with aging and choose continual cosmetic surgery to circumvent this we are not legitimately aging. We are saying that we do not like ourselves unless we are young. True self-esteem involves the choice to accept the aging process as part of our development and learning. We sometimes do not choose legitimate suffering or make wise choices for self-worth because we adopted poor models.

The Presence of Good Models

Models are important for early self-esteem development. *Models for children are most often adults or older children. Models are extremely important when we are young because we adopt the behaviors and attitudes we attribute to these models.*

Adults serve as models in three important ways—what we say, what we do, and who we are. Children hear and see how we experience our own self-worth by hearing us talk. For example, if we work hard to prepare a meal for visitors and we are given compliments on how good the food is, what do we say? If we say, "Oh it was nothing," we are sending the message that we can work hard and then demean our efforts by not taking appropriate credit for it. This gives children a clear signal that we feel unworthy. If someone gives us a compliment for good work, the appropriate response is, "Thank you."

What we do is more important than what we say. If we tell children it is important to be honest and then tell "little white lies" then our example is what really counts. The old adage "actions speak louder than words" is true. If we say to children "you are somebody" and do not show that we are somebody, then they see the emptiness in the words and follow our actions.

The most important model for self-esteem is who we are. This is ultimately reflected in what we say and what we do. Who we are is very difficult to hide from children. Anyone who has worked with preschoolers knows how they can pick up on what irritates us or pushes our buttons quicker than adults can. They may see in us low self-esteem, even when other adults cannot.

A *sense of belonging, a feeling of individuality, the ability to choose wisely,* and *the adoption or representation of good models are all important to high self-regard.* How we experience these is always individual. We do know much about how and where we get them. This is the next focus for our discussion—*where we get our self-esteem.*

WHERE DO WE GET OUR SELF-ESTEEM?

Self-esteem is constructed from inside each person through interacting with others and the environment. This inside construction is derived from many different sources. These sources influence us by interacting with one another to such a degree that it is often difficult to decipher just how these interactions take place. We often do not see the many things which interact to produce self-esteem. It is much like chemical compounds. When we combine two parts hydrogen with one part oxygen, we come up with water. We do not see the hydrogen or the oxygen; we see water.

Of the many things which interact to direct our self-esteem, eight of them are extremely important. These include the influence of 1) *others*, 2) *institutions*, 3) *personalities*, 4) *experiences*, 5) *history*, 6) *environments and social class*, 7) *our cultural heritage*, and 8) *our decisions*.

The Influence of Others
Other people constantly have an impact on our self-worth. As babies our parents' influence has the greatest effect on our devel-

opment. They hold the keys to food, clothing, and shelter, and our first experiences with self-regard are directed by them. The experience with self-worth is largely unconscious at first. Infants have a sense of how adults feel about them and how comfortable the adults are with themselves. Very early in life we are spontaneous, uninhibited, and without any concern for impressing others. We do not yet have the ability to consider what others think of us. During this time, how our parents accept, reward, or punish us makes a difference in how we learn to accept ourselves.

The responses of our parents, others, and the environment give us a feeling of control or lack of it. Infants who cry continually without anyone ever responding begin to feel they have no control over their environment. Anything they do does not seem to make any difference. Parents who respond to their children's needs help them feel they have some control over their world.

Soon other people begin to make a difference. Day care workers, baby sitters, and siblings have an early effect on us. The mirror of how we learn to see and value ourselves is passed around to others to help form the images and feelings we construct.

By the time we enter school a collection of people have influenced us. Our teachers are important in early elementary school, and then we pay a lot of attention to our friends and peers in middle and high school. By adulthood our intimate relationships tell us much about who we are. The people at work such as our boss and colleagues shape us too. Soon our own children and grandchildren share in the development of how we regard ourselves. *There is no life which is not influenced by how others respond to them.* Many people base their self-worth on the value others attribute to them.

The Influence of Institutions

By institutions I am referring to a collection of others that can be named. School, Boy Scouts, church, synagogue, the Junior League, the Masonic Lodge, a bridge club are all examples of institutions which might interact with us. Sometimes our institutions conflict with one another and this creates tension. Piano lessons and football practice may compete for our attention and stretch how we define and feel about ourselves.

Institutions invariably involve competition within and between them. Competition, comparison, and conformity are inherent in many of our institutions. How we interact with institutions and accept successes and disappointments within the institutions we participate in contributes much to our developing self-regard.

The Influence of Personalities

Our self-worth is also affected by our personality type. Some of us are more extroverted than others. Some people pay close attention to the outside world while others tend to spend time on their inner worlds. Some folks make their decisions mostly from the head while others value the heart. Some of us have a strong need for structure and order, while others do not.

How our personality is honored and valued is important. I have heard adults ask introverted children, "What's the matter? Cat got your tongue?" I have seen children severely punished for having a messy room. When we relate to children or other adults, we need to respect their personality traits. Throughout life we are unique in personality. We have to learn how to live in society and relate to others, but at the same time we can accept and value what makes each of us different.

The Influence of Experiences

What happens to us early in life affects us later. We all remember painful experiences which adjusted our self-esteem. How we react to these experiences over time is individual. One experience will devastate someone while the same type of experience will be an impetus for another to overcome the trauma.

Experience is the builder of high self-esteem if we are paying attention. *Experience is the major portion of the spiral of self-esteem which keeps posing issues and problems for us to face.*

We face the same dilemmas continually until we hopefully have developed self-esteem in the face of them. Rachel has had terrible experiences with men and has low self-regard for her ability to develop male/female intimate relationships. What Rachel may not realize is that she interacts with these experiences to help produce her self-esteem. How she reacts will make a difference. Each new experience she has with men brings the opportunity for her to learn more about herself and how she contributes to her own lack of self-worth.

Over time we learn it is not so much what happens to us but what happens inside us which shapes us. Some of our experiences we have no control over, but we can learn to love ourselves in the presence of all adversity. Experiences will spiral around to us again, if only in memories until we learn to deal with them.

The Influence of History

History of all types contributes to who we become—personal history, family history, cultural history, and even national history. It is easier to see how personal history or family history concerns us. Our cultural and national heritage are contributors as well. Most women born in the 1800s were considered second class citizens and as the property of their husband or families. This general lack of regard for women's worth impacted on their self-esteem.

Even today, senior adult women may have chosen their place or defined themselves in terms of their husbands. Even younger women have experienced an inferior place in the culture. I was recently looking at a small town high school annual (yearbook) from the 1970s. I was surprised to see the female teachers' names were that of their husbands—Mrs. John Jones or Mrs. Keith Smith. These women all had jobs as teachers but were still identified by their husbands' names. I am not implying that it is wrong for women to take their husband's names. I am suggesting, however, there is a choice, but history and culture have shown that this was not always a choice.

The Impact of Environments and Social Class

Some environments are more stressful than others. Individuals raised in poorer neighborhoods may see crimes, poverty, and stressors of which others may not be aware. Such situations may create fears and feelings of helplessness. This does not mean that people raised in poorer homes will have lower self-esteem; it means that our environments and social class contribute to our self-regard. Opportunities to become all we can be take resources which are sometimes beyond our control.

Adolescence is a difficult time for those from lower income families. Clothing, clubs, transportation, parties, and the prom may tax family resources. Teens who get their self-worth predominantly from popularity may feel worthless if they do not have resources for such experiences.

Senior citizens who find themselves in poverty or low standard nursing homes may question their self-regard as well. We can work toward developing positive attitudes beyond our environment, but the places we find ourselves contribute to how we construct our self-esteem.

The Influence of the Culture

The culture of which we are a part "makes recommendations" for how we should see and like ourselves. When we hear slogans like "You can never be too rich or too thin" we know our culture has a rating system for self-worth. We find our culture values youth, athletes, scientists, and the list goes on. Many cultures encourage young people to major in the sciences instead of the arts. What does that say for artists?

We don't have to buy into our culture's ideas of what makes people worthwhile, but it takes a tremendous amount of liking ourselves to transcend these cultural ideas.

Since America is the land of many cultures, conflicting cultural values can also do a number on our self-esteem. We were founded on the idea of religious freedom, yet it was 1978 before Native

Americans were given the right to full religious freedom. What message were Native Americans given about their worth? What does this tell us about our own self-esteem? This issue of culture is so vital to individual self-esteem that I have written much about it throughout this book.

The Influence of Our Decisions

There are so many things which interact in the development of self-regard we sometimes feel we have no control over it. Early in life we have limited control. Adults hold many keys to our development including some to our self-esteem. As we grow older we are allowed more and more control over the decisions we make which includes the decision of how we will love ourselves. Unfortunately, many of us do not realize we have this ability.

In early childhood we watched how our parents, siblings, teachers, and friends acted, and sometimes we decided to copy their behaviors. More important, though, was how we decided our own worth through these relationships.

One way some of us decided we could get self-esteem was by buying it from others. When we took the teacher an apple and thought she liked us because of the gift we decided to give apples for our self-esteem. These apples became more and more sophisticated. We learned how to flatter our spouse or take our boss to lunch in order to get self-esteem. Such decisions to buy self-esteem from others work only so long. During midlife we realize this isn't working like we thought it would. Purchasing love is an important theme which will be discussed in detail in chapter eight. We can all learn how to make better decisions for loving ourselves and others.

Self-esteem comes from deep inside us. Belonging, uniqueness, choices, and models are all necessary for constructing and building it. Others, institutions, our personality, experiences, history, environments, social class, and culture all interact and are taken into consideration when we decide who we are and how we like what we see inside.

Chapter Two

DEVELOPING SELF-ESTEEM IN INFANTS AND TODDLERS

(BIRTH THROUGH AGE THREE)

The foundation for self-esteem is determined in the earliest years of life. What happens from birth through age three sets the stage for later self-esteem. Several experiences are important for the young child's developing sense of self. These include (1) *the development of bonding and attachment,* (2) *adult acceptance of the child's temperament,* (3) *the child's development of trust and autonomy,* (4) *the effects of the parents' self-esteem,* (5) *the adult's understanding of stranger and separation anxiety,* and (6) *the child's mastery of developmental tasks* (such as walking, talking, or potty training).

THE DEVELOPMENT OF BONDING AND ATTACHMENT

Bonding and attachment are necessary for a baby's sense of security. Just what is *bonding* and what is *attachment?* Bonding is a feeling of closeness and connectedness that is enhanced by a close proximity between a mother and her child shortly after birth. A mother's attitude toward her baby may partly depend on experiences with the child shortly after birth.

Babies who are more responsive to their parents help the parents feel affectionate toward them. For example, a baby who looks at the mother attentively and snuggles to her helps the mother bond to the child. However, if there is limited contact between mother and child or if the child is unresponsive or continually upset, bonding may be hampered.

As the baby has more and more contact with the parents, **attachment** begins. Attachment is a close emotional tie that develops and is enduring over time. Back in the 1960s, the famous researchers, Dr. Rudolph Schaffer and Dr. Peggy Emerson, found that Scottish babies pass through several stages in their development of attachment. These include **the asocial stage** (up to six weeks) in which the child responds to most anyone. From about six weeks to six or seven months a baby passes through the **indiscriminate attachment stage** in which she likes to be around people, but it often does not matter if the people are strangers. The **specific attachment stage** occurs around seven months when the child prefers a specific person such as the mother or caregiver. Finally by eighteen months of age the child is in the **multiple attachments stage** where she may be attached to siblings and as many as five or more people.

Since the time of Drs. Schaffer and Emerson, other researchers have found that babies are more discriminating in their attachments even earlier than six or seven months. The point here is that strong secure attachments are a necessary foundation for a child's development of self-esteem. Problems in the development of attachment may influence later self-worth.

What problems exist in a baby's development of attachments? Dr. David R. Shaffer, a psychologist at the University of Georgia, says three problem situations affect attachments. He points out that 1) *some babies are difficult,* 2) *some parents are difficult,* and 3) *some environments are difficult.*

Premature babies are more difficult because they are sometimes unresponsive to the attention of the parents and caregivers. They are more inalert than full term babies and spend more of their time crying. Some need intensive care which separates them more from the parents than is the case with full term babies. Also, a baby's *temperament* may prove difficult for some parents. A good match between the baby's *temperament* and the parents' personalities is important. *Temperament* will be described later in this chapter.

Parents can also be deficient in their ability to achieve appropriate attachments. Parents who have difficulties interacting with their babies include parents who are chronically depressed, those who were unloved, abused, or neglected, those who have preconceived ideas about what a baby should be like, and those for whatever reason do not want their babies. The development of attachment is important for the infant's self-esteem development.

Suzanne is an example of a mother who had great difficulty with attachment. She and her husband Phil had been married for twenty years before she became pregnant. Suzanne had lived a very structured and ordered life. She had developed such a need for order that she spent a considerable amount of time arranging her clothes and lived for many years with a predictably rigid schedule. When her daughter was born she wanted to place her on a schedule too. She had decided that the baby would eat at a specific time of day and sleep at a particular time. Suzanne was shocked to find that her newborn, Carole, did not conform to this schedule. Carole was hungry at different times and did not sleep on Suzanne's time table. This created problems with attachment and Suzanne had to seek professional help to better understand herself and her baby.

Babies like Carole who feel they have no control over their environment may stop trying and develop what Dr. M. E. Seligman refers to as *learned helplessness*. Parents can also feel helpless when their efforts to soothe a baby are continually unsuccessful. They may have doubts about their abilities as parents and stop trying.

Besides the parents and the child, certain *environments* are not helpful to the development of attachment and self-esteem. For example, mothers who have to care for their newborn with little or no help may not have time to devote to the child. Further, the more children a single mother has, the less available time she has to spend with each child.

Also, parents who are unhappy in their marriage may communicate this unconsciously to their infants. Babies are able to pick up the emotional atmosphere of the house. If parents are unhappy and do not feel good about themselves their baby will pick up on this.

Since more and more mothers have entered the work force, more and more infants and toddlers are spending their earlier years in day care or child care centers. The quality of care provided in these settings will also have an important influence on the child's developing sense of self-worth.

ACCEPTANCE OF THE CHILD'S TEMPERAMENT

We are all born with certain personality traits. This is what makes us individual. How parents accept the newborn's temperament will make a big difference in the baby's developing self-esteem. Just what is *temperament?* Temperament is simply the inborn part of the personality. Each child is born with unique temperament characteristics which include responses, emotions, and interactions with others—right from day one!

In their famous book *Temperament and Development*, Drs. Alexander Thomas and S. Chess report that babies differ in at least nine personality or temperament traits. Remember that this is inborn and can be easily seen during the first few months of life. The following are the nine temperament traits which Drs. Thomas and Chess report are different in every child:

1. *Activity level.* Some babies are more active than others. They move around while others are more sedate.
2. *Rhythmicity*. Some babies are more predictable in their rhythms. They sleep, eat, and even eliminate fairly predictably.

Other babies are much less predictable.

3. *Approach-Withdrawal.* Some infants and toddlers are much better at accepting new things than others. Examples would be in trying new foods, getting the first haircut, or taking the first bath. Some will cry and be difficult; others will laugh and enjoy.

4. *Adaptability.* Some babies insist on a regular routine. Others adjust to changing routines and people.

5. *Intensity of reaction.* Some babies whimper while others scream out loud. Some chuckle loudly while others simply smile. Each baby has his own intenseness in reacting.

6. *Threshold of responsiveness.* Some babies are more aware of sights and sounds than others. Their response to sensations is partially due to this threshold.

7. *Quality of mood.* Some babies are happier than others. Some smile at almost anything while others are much more difficult in their mood.

8. *Distractibility.* Some babies are single-minded and not easily distracted. When they are hungry, nothing will do until they are fed. Others are more distractible. When angry they may forget their anger when handed a rattle.

9. *Attention span.* Some babies will look at their mobile for long periods of time while others have a more limited attention span.

What does temperament have to do with the development of healthy self-esteem? How parents and caregivers respond to a child's temperament influences that child's understanding of whether or not she is OK. Parental reactions to temperament serve as the early mirror reflecting back to the child her valued worth.

Dr. T. Berry Brazelton, one of the country's leading pediatricians, talks about easy babies and difficult babies. Even within a household of two small children, one may be easy while the other may be more difficult. Accepting both children and valuing each one's individuality is a basic foundation for their developing self-esteem.

THE CHILD'S DEVELOPMENT OF
TRUST AND AUTONOMY

During infancy and toddlerhood, a child goes through two psychosocial dilemmas according to psychoanalyst Erik Erikson. These include *trust versus mistrust* and *autonomy versus shame or doubt.* In early infancy the child needs a safe environment in which her basic needs are met. If inconsistent or inadequate care occur then the child is much more likely to distrust others and the environment.

A lack of trust can be avoided if parents will provide sameness and consistency in the environment. John, a thirty-one-year-old construction worker, was raised in a loving middle class home. He reports a lack of trust in others. When discussing this with his parents, he found that his family had moved to another community during his first year of life. The house they were to move into was not finished so they stayed in a motel for three months. His mother said he became sick, but the pediatrician could find nothing physically wrong with him. The pediatrician suggested providing some familiar objects and surroundings for John while they were still living in the motel. His parents unpacked some of the household items which were familiar to John and he immediately improved. Whether or not John's lack of trust can be traced back to this incident is questionable. However, the first year of life is extremely important for a person's development of trust. With an increasingly mobile society it appears important to provide as much continuity and sameness as possible during the first year of life.

Around the second or third year of life the dilemmas a child faces is *autonomy versus shame.* A child who is allowed to explore and try out her new skills such as walking will more likely develop a sense of autonomy than the child who is overprotected. Overprotective parents give the child the view that the world is a terribly unsafe place to live. During this age it is especially important to childproof the home by removing dangerous chemicals from lower cabinets as well as temporarily moving the fine china (or breakable or dangerous objects) from the living areas of the house.

Children who feel secure and trusting will more likely explore the environment and develop a sense of autonomy and spontaneity. The development of self-esteem requires a certain trust of others and the environment as well as a feeling of autonomy.

THE IMPORTANCE OF THE PARENTS' SELF-ESTEEM

The caregivers are the primary contributors in the drama of self-development during infancy and toddlerhood. How the mother and father interact with the child sets the wheels of self-esteem in motion. This would also be true of day care workers or child care providers when the child is placed in day care before the age of three.

Why is the parent's self-esteem so important? According to Swiss psychologist Dr. Carl Jung a child's individual development is only partially present at birth. The mother's unconscious is strongly attached to the infant's unconscious. This means that the child's initial self-esteem is in essence that of the mother's self-esteem.

Some psychologists disagree with Dr. Jung concerning this unconscious connection, but they still give credence to the importance of the parent's actions on the child's self-esteem. Young children imitate or model their parents' behaviors. If the parents demonstrate low self-esteem, the child is more likely to copy this low self-worth.

Parents with low self-esteem also tend to be overprotective at a time when the child needs to explore the environment and develop autonomy. Parents with low self-esteem tend to see a problem in everything and give the child the idea that the world is a terrible place to live.

Jayne is a young mother who has great doubts about her mothering abilities. One thing she is determined about is that her three-year-old son will not develop low self-esteem as she has. While this is a commendable attitude, what she does not yet realize is that

her own self-esteem is being imitated by her son. She is constant-
ly afraid he will fall and hurt himself. Since she wants to be a good
mother and feels guilt about her own inadequacy she seeks to do
everything for the child at the expense of his learning about the
world through his own explorations and mistakes. As a result, her
son has already begun to doubt his own abilities and is now afraid
to try out new things. Jayne needs to work on her own self-esteem
which will, in turn, improve her relationship with her son and hope-
fully allow him the freedom to explore.

UNDERSTANDING STRANGER ANXIETY AND SEPARATION ANXIETY

Two normal developmental milestones should be considered in
terms of self-esteem. These include *stranger anxiety* and *separation
anxiety*. Babies normally develop stranger anxiety around the age
of six to seven months which peaks around ten months and then
gradually decreases throughout the second year of life. Separation
anxiety (distress about being away from the mother) usually emerges
around seven to twelve months and peaks at about fourteen to twen-
ty months becoming less intense throughout toddlerhood and the
preschool years, according to Dr. Shaffer of the University of
Georgia.

What makes an infant afraid of a stranger? Many things influence
whether a baby will be frightened by someone new. Besides the
baby's temperament, such things as the presence of the parent, the
familiarity of the place where the stranger is encountered, how the
stranger acts toward the infant, and the stranger's size and physical
characteristics all contribute to whether or not a stranger will be a
source of distress in the young child.

Fifteen-month-old Andrew appeared happy to see a middle-aged
man when he visited the home of Andrew's parents. However,
when Andrew's mother went to the back of the house to get some-
thing and left Andrew for a short time with his father and the

stranger, Andrew became distressed. He showed very normal signs of both stranger and separation anxiety. At first Andrew took the stranger man's hand and tried to lead him to the back where Andrew's mother was. When this did not work, he became afraid of the man and ran to his father.

Andrew's parents are very familiar with the phenomenon of stranger anxiety and separation anxiety. Andrew's father has a PhD in early childhood development and knew how to soothe Andrew until his mother returned to the room. This was important for Andrew's sense of security and self-esteem because his father accepted Andrew's reactions as a normal part of Andrew's maturation. Had the father not known about stranger or separation anxiety and tried to force Andrew to interact with the man or scolded him for wanting his mother, Andrew might have begun to develop doubts about his feelings (especially if this episode was repeated numerous times over the course of infancy and toddlerhood).

THE CHILD'S MASTERY OF DEVELOPMENTAL TASKS

One of the most interesting topics of toddlerhood is potty training. This is just one example of many skills which are developing during the first three years of life. Others include talking, walking, and feeling. The support and encouragement the young child receives for attempts at each are vital to feelings of self-regard. More important, though, is the lack of pressure imposed on the child to achieve these milestones.

Parents should be very leery of books with titles such as *Potty Train Your Child in One Easy Lesson* or *Teach Your Baby to Read by the Time He is Three*. Normal children are very capable of developing at their own speed without coercion from adults. The need for a child to walk, talk, or read early is the need of the parents and not the child. This is especially true of potty training. Some parents who are expecting another child when they already have a two

year old want to make sure the two year old is potty trained before
the new baby arrives. This is indeed the parents' need and not the
baby's. In fact, many two year olds are not physically capable of
retaining feces or urine even if they wanted to.

Just what does the mastery of skills and developmental mile-
stones have to do with self-esteem? Once again, the young child who
is pushed to do something she is not yet capable of undermines her
sense of self-worth. It is important to note here that the younger
the child the less we can predict her future development. Remember
that Einstein did not talk until very late and other great scientists and
artists were also developmentally delayed.

In Western cultures there is often no room for late bloomers.
When I talk to parents about self-esteem I always refer to the book
Leo the Late Bloomer by Robert Kraus. It should be required read-
ing for every parent. Children in the United States are branded or
labeled as being slow as early as one year of age when they may, in
fact, just be late bloomers. Because a first child talked at eleven
months of age and the second child did not speak in words until
fifteen months does not necessarily indicate that the first child is
smarter or will have an easier life. The bottom line is children
should be supported and encouraged for their efforts but not pushed
or forced beyond their abilities. This pushing creates an antithetical
relationship between parents and child and interrupts the dance of
synchronicity.

THE DANCE OF SYNCHRONICITY

Have you ever wondered why people who know nothing about
children raise their children to become healthy, productive, respon-
sible adults with high self-esteem? The answer lies partly in that
infants are very capable of communicating with us in their own
way. They are able to let us know what their needs are if we will just
pay attention. When a newborn is crying at the top of her lungs we
see if she is hungry, or sleepy, or wet, or hurting. Most mothers

will tell you that they can tell right away what the cry of their baby means. This is important to the baby's self-esteem development. *If we can just relax and enjoy the baby's development and pay attention to what she is trying to tell us, we will be on the way to providing a safe place for the baby to feel good.*

There is a certain dance between a parent and child that takes place if the parents will just pay attention. The child communicates something and then we respond. This interaction goes back and forth and provides a certain synchronicity like ballroom dancing.

SOME MORE PRACTICAL CONCRETE SUGGESTIONS

Since the idea of self-esteem is so abstract it is difficult to even talk about it in terms of infancy and toddlerhood. Yet, so much of what we do with children this age influences their future self-esteem development. The following additional suggestions are made to help a child on her journey toward high self-esteem based on what we have considered in this chapter.

1. Talk to a baby frequently during the first three years of life and "listen" to what the child is communicating.
2. Accept the baby's temperament and do not try to impose set ideas about what the child should be like. Remember that children in the same family have different temperaments and because an older sibling was an easy baby does not mean that the next one should be. Avoid making comparisons.
3. Provide as much sameness, consistency, and adequate care as possible so that the infant will develop trusting relationships.
4. Childproof the home and develop an environment which is safe for the toddler to explore.
5. Accept the toddler's need for exploration and avoid overprotectiveness while the child tries out new skills.

6. Work on your own self-esteem since very young children pick up either consciously or unconsciously the feelings adults have about themselves.

7. Choose good caregivers and babysitters who also feel good about themselves and are comfortable working with infants and toddlers.

8. Understand that it is normal for children to pass through both stranger and separation anxiety. Do not shame a child for exhibiting such characteristics and avoid placing them in situations which create undue anxiety.

9. Enjoy the child's mastery of such skills as talking, walking, feeding, and potty training. Above all, do not push the child to accomplish things beyond her abilities because you have a need to have a smart baby.

10. Above all, enjoy the infant and toddler and take pride in their development, no matter how delayed or accelerated. This period passes so fast the best way we can lay a foundation for self-esteem is to (as much as possible) simply relax and enjoy it.

OTHER RESOURCES TO HELP YOU FOLLOW UP WHAT YOU LEARNED IN THIS CHAPTER

Briggs, Dorothy Corkille. *Your Child's Self-esteem.* New York: Doubleday, 1970.

Everything from a child's safety to ways of disciplining are described to help parents build self-esteem in their infants and toddlers.

Curry, Nancy E., and Johnson, Carl N. *Beyond Self-esteem.* Washington, DC: NAEYC Press, 1990.

This book was written for parents, teachers, administrators, and policy makers who work with very young children. Self-esteem is described in the larger context of the child's environment as well as the child's own personality, cognitive, and moral development.

Greenberg, Polly. *Character Development: Encouraging Self-esteem and Self-discipline in Infants, Toddlers, and Two Year Olds.* Washington, DC: NAEYC Press, 1991.

Parents, family child care providers, and infant-toddler teachers can learn ways to foster self-esteem in babies through communicating with them and teaching them at their individually appropriate levels.

CHAPTER THREE

DEVELOPING SELF-ESTEEM IN EARLY CHILDHOOD

(THREE THROUGH SIX)

The ages of three through six are extremely important to the development of self-esteem. It is during this time that children learn much about the world through taking initiative and continuing to explore the environment. An understanding of how children develop at this age is necessary to help build self-esteem.

An interesting fact about self-esteem is that we learn by doing, especially during this age. It is the time we begin to really develop specific areas of self-esteem. A good example is language development. I often ask students in my college classes, "How many of you think you are good writers?" (meaning writing poetry, short stories, novels, etc., instead of penmanship). Very few raise their hands to this question. Then I ask, "How many of you think you are good talkers?" They all raise their hands. We can infer from this that many adults have high self-esteem for talking but low self-esteem for writing. How did this happen? It began during this period from three through six years of age. No one was born with the idea that they were good talkers but poor writers, so let's see how this happened.

When most of us were babies and began saying, "da da" or "ma ma" our parents were thrilled. They were not upset because we were not yet speaking in complete sentences. No parent says to a baby, "No, you can't say 'da da' you must say 'I want my daddy'." Our parents let us go through the stages of cooing and babbling and encouraged us. What happened? We all learned to talk and feel pretty good about it.

Unfortunately this was not the case when we started experimenting with writing or spelling. Most of us were told when we picked up a pencil or a crayon that we must stay within the lines and write correctly and neatly. During the preschool years children need to go through developmental stages of writing just as they go through developmental stages of talking. Babies go through cooing, babbling, and other stages in developing speech. They also pass through the stages of scribbling and pretend writing during preschool. Allowing them to do so is necessary if they are ever to feel good about their writing abilities.

When children begin to play with writing it is almost always scribbling at first. Later we see shapes appear in their writing, and eventually we find one or two familiar letters used to represent the spelling of a word. It is not until the elementary grades that we begin to seriously help them edit their writing if they are to feel good about their early efforts.

So, it is during the early childhood years that we often begin to feel good in some areas (like talking) and not so good about ourselves in other areas (like writing). Most of this has to do with how adults treat talking and writing.

The same thing is true for drawing or painting. I also ask my classes, "How many of you think of yourselves as artists?" Again, very few of them ever raise their hands. Where did they get the idea that they could not draw or create? This probably occurred during the preschool years. When children start to experiment with drawing, they scribble. It is often not until children are five or six that adults begin to see recognizable drawings. How we treat children's early efforts at writing and drawing influences their specific self-esteem in these areas.

Since the development of self-esteem is so important at this age it is necessary to look at what adults do that is detrimental to its development. Two sources which tell us much about this are Dr. David Elkind's book *The Hurried Child* and Drs. Maryann and Gary Manning's article "The School's Assault on Childhood" from *Childhood Education.*

Dr. Elkind mentions several ways we hurry children which include clothing, activity, lack of reading to them, and information. Children are being hurried with regard to the clothing they wear. Specifically, it is difficult today to tell the difference between adult and childhood clothing. There are even designer diapers for infants. Preschoolers are wearing make-up. Early childhood is a distinct period in which children do not need to be grown up.

More devastating to self-esteem development are the activities in which young children are engaged. For example, there is now "Little Miss Shopping Mall" with a competitive division for three, four, and five year olds. Sometimes these pageants even have a category for infants.

Marilyn is an ambitious housewife and mother with a three-year-old daughter named Karen. Marilyn always wanted to be the homecoming queen and her state's representative to Miss America. She never had the opportunity to participate in pageants and did not make the homecoming court in high school. She now enters Karen in every beauty pageant that comes along. Karen is not even sure what is going on, but she doesn't want to be in pageants. Because of this she gets a lecture from Marilyn. She tells her daughter about never having the chance to be in contests so Karen should really be thankful (a lecture far beyond Karen's capacity to comprehend). Of the four pageants Karen has been entered she has not won any prizes, and although she doesn't really understand what is happening, she is losing, and she knows her mother is disappointed. The whole pageant idea is Marilyn's need and not Karen's.

Girls are not the only ones being hurried by developmentally inappropriate activities. Ron is a thirty-five-year-old computer programmer who was the star of the football team in high school. He has never been a major success in his job and yearns for the good old days of high school football. His four-year-old son, Paul, has been enrolled in a peewee football team with uniforms, coaches, and the works. Ron is very encouraging to Paul, and Paul wants to please his dad very much. However, when Paul screws up on the field during a game his father goes down to the fence and yells at his son, telling him that he can do better than that. Once again, it is Ron's need for football glory and not Paul's. After all, Paul is just four years old and needs the activity of spontaneous, unstructured play before being thrown to the wolves by his father.

Another way we hurry children is in the way we treat reading. Carol began using flashcards years ago with her five-year-old Mark (almost before he could sit up in his crib). She had read a book about teaching her baby to read by the time he was three and is anxious to show his reading ability to the family and neighbors. What she should be doing is reading good books to Mark every day and helping him enjoy simple predictable books and fairytales and folktales. Mark is not learning the flashcards as quickly as Carol thinks he should, and they are both frustrated.

Information given to children can also influence their feelings of worth. Ted and Barbara allow their three- and five-year-old daughters to see R-rated movies on cable television. Ted and Barbara are also having severe marital difficulties and are considering a divorce. They shout at each other in front of the children and discuss each other with their friends on the telephone in front of their daughters. Such information is creating a frightening atmosphere for the daughters who both have trouble sleeping at night. The five year old is even afraid that all the trouble is her fault even though she really does not understand what is going on.

Dr. Elkind is certainly correct when he describes the ways we hurry children through clothing, activity, reading, and information. All of this hurrying has a devastating influence on preschoolers' self-esteem development.

Drs. Maryann and Gary Manning of the University of Alabama at Birmingham have described how schools assault young children. Although their concerns include children from ages six through eight, their ideas are even more true today for preschoolers. These concerns include drill, worksheets, fragmentation, homogeneous grouping, and long periods of sitting and listening in preschool programs. They are also concerned about the heavy emphasis on testing preschoolers. All of these activities which schools impose on children undermine a child's development of healthy self-esteem.

The emphasis on drilling children can be seen in both the family and preschool settings. Clara is a proud grandmother of John, a three year old who lives next door to her. When Clara's friends come to visit her she sends for her grandson John. John is attending a highly structured preschool which drills children like the military. When John arrives, Clara always asked John to do three things for her. First, John is to count to thirty from memory. Then he has to say his ABC's. Finally, John has to quote the 23rd Psalm from the Bible. John seems quite happy to accommodate his grandmother. However, he doesn't have a clue about what he is doing. Sometimes Clara's friends ask John to do something like count three blocks. John doesn't understand. He can rote count to thirty but cannot count three blocks. If John is asked to identify the letter "b" he doesn't know what that means even though he can say all of the alphabet. If John is asked what the 23rd Psalm means, he doesn't have a clue. It is clear that John has been *drilled* to memorize his numbers, alphabet, and Bible verses. All of this rote memorization is teaching John very early in life that all knowledge comes from the heads of adults and if he wants to be a good boy he must do things he does not understand. While he enjoys the applause and praise of his grandmother and other adults, the long-range effects of this drilling will be for him to depend on others for approval and learning and not rely on his own initiative. John is learning early to rely on others for his self-esteem.

A lot of preschool programs rely heavily on paper and pencil activities such as color sheets, coloring books, workbooks or worksheets. Preschoolers learn by hands-on activities and not worksheets. The best learning in preschool involves hands-on materials and physical activity. If we want a preschooler to learn about apples, we bring in apples, we eat them, and we make applesauce. Preschoolers learn so much more from this than they would a coloring book full of apples. Sometimes it is difficult to have hands-on experiences. A giraffe or elephant make a good example. In these cases we can take children to the zoo so that they can have a first hand experience with animals. The next best thing would be a model or a picture. If we cannot take a preschooler on an airplane ride we can show a model, picture, or a film of an airplane, or we can set up a model airplane in the housekeeping center so that children can pretend to go on an airplane ride. The most abstract thing of all for a preschooler would be imposed paper and pencil activities. We do children a disservice when all of their time is spent using paper and pencil. This is also true of coloring sheets. Children who are given coloring books and expected to stay within the lines are at-risk in self-esteem development.

This is also true of art projects. I once went in a preschool classroom where the teacher had made a sheep out of cottonballs on construction paper. Three cottonballs made up the face and six made up the body. The children were expected to make their sheep exactly like the teacher's model and not create their own. There were fifteen children in the room but only four sheep were on display. I asked the teacher if every child had made a sheep and she responded, "Oh, yes, but only four were good enough to put on the wall. The others were either messy or did not follow instructions. I simply tore them up in front of the children as a lesson to them.

They should learn to follow directions if they want their work shown in this room!"

The same teacher told me that Susan was a bad girl. She had colored a cow green even though she knew better. (Naturally, Susan was sitting there listening to this story.)

Just what does all of this have to do with self-esteem? There is now a room full of preschoolers who think they cannot color, they cannot make good sheep, and the implications for their self-esteem development (at least in the area of art) are obvious.

Another assault which the Mannings mention is *fragmentation.* Just what is fragmentation? Fragmentation is a lot of starting and stopping of activities during the day.

Carla is a four year old enrolled in a fast-paced preschool program. Her teacher, Ms. Sparks, believes that she is an innovative teacher. She has learning centers set up around the room for children to move around during the day. Ms. Sparks rings a bell every ten minutes so the children will move to the next learning station. A group of visitors came to Ms. Sparks' class to observe how she used learning centers. Carla was at the block center when the visitors were in the room. One of the visitors asked Carla, "Don't you want to build something with blocks?" Carla answered, "Oh no! I won't have time. Ms. Sparks will ring the bell, and I'll have to go somewhere else." Carla has already learned that she doesn't have time in life to do anything for she will soon have to move somewhere else.

An almost opposite extreme also occurs in Ms. Sparks' classroom. The children spend over an hour in circle time sitting and listening to the teacher talk about the calendar, the weather, reading stories out loud, having the children come up and find their names on a chart, etc. The problem during circle time is that it is too long and children are asked to sit and listen for a period of time which is not appropriate for preschoolers. It seems that the children are not spending enough time (for individual activities) and too much time (for large group activities).

OTHER RESOURCES TO HELP YOU FOLLOW UP WHAT YOU HAVE LEARNED IN THIS CHAPTER

Aldridge, Jerry. "Helping children build self-esteem." *Day Care and Early Education*, 17(2), pp.4-7, 1989.

This article describes four requirements for high self-esteem in early childhood. Seven suggestions are given for improving a young child's self-esteem.

Bredekamp, Sue. *Developmentally Appropriate Practice in Early Childhood Programs Serving Children From Birth Through Age 8*. Washington, DC: NAEYC Press, 1987.

Children in preschools, kindergartens, and early elementary schools should be enrolled in programs which are developmentally appropriate. This booklet describes self-esteem activities which are both age and individually appropriate.

Elkind, David. *The Hurried Child*. Reading, MA: Addison-Wesley, 1981.

Dr. Elkind describes *how* we hurry children, *how* this influences their self-esteem, and *what* we can do about it.

Manning, Maryann, and Manning, Gary. "The school's assault on childhood." *Childhood Education*, 57(2), pp. 84-87, 1981.

This article describes six school practices which are harmful to a child's self-esteem.

Neumann, Erich. *The Child*. Boston: Shambhala, 1973.

The importance of the parent-child relationship to self-esteem is explained.

Wickes, Frances. *The Inner World of Childhood*. London: Coventure, 1927.

Dr. Wickes describes how a child's personality and inner world of fantasy are related to self-worth development.

CHAPTER FOUR

DEVELOPING SELF-ESTEEM IN MIDDLE CHILDHOOD
(SIX THROUGH NINE)

There is no doubt that school becomes a major influence in a child's self-esteem during grades one through three. In this chapter we will consider (1) *the impact of schooling on self-worth,* (2) *the importance of the parent and school partnership,* (3) *the effects of stress on self-esteem,* and (4) t*he continuing development of individuality* .

THE IMPACT OF SCHOOLING

During the preschool years the parents and child care providers have a strong impact on a child's self-esteem. Now that the child is in the primary grades, there is an ever-widening circle of influences on self-worth which includes teachers and peers. The importance of the teacher on self-esteem during this time cannot be overstressed.

The great psychologist Erik Erikson describes this as the industrious time of child development, meaning the child likes to learn and make things and be recognized for such efforts. If the child's efforts are not valued then a feeling of inferiority sets in.

A child in early elementary school is usually eager to please the teacher. The child is willing to give up her autonomy and even integrity sometimes to fulfill the need to please. Ms. Jackson is a first grade teacher who knows this and uses it somewhat negatively for her own amusement. For example she told her class, "When Ms. Ray (another first grade teacher) comes into our room, everyone raise both hands over your heads." The children, who were willing to please Ms. Jackson, do so without question, simply because her approval is important to them.

The Oak School is an example of just how powerful a primary level teacher's expectations can influence children's achievement and self-esteem. In a now classic experiment, teachers were told that some children in their room had unusual potential. Actually, the children were just chosen at random. The teachers did not do anything special for these children in terms of spending time with them or extra instruction. However, many of these children showed significant IQ gains. The idea of self-fulfilling prophecy was at work. Self-fulfilling prophecy means that children live up to the expectations others have of them.

Teachers can also have a negative impact on children's self-regard, especially when the teachers do not have a clear understanding of normal child development. I once received a phone call from a principal of an elementary school who was concerned because the first grade teachers in his school were failing children on spelling tests. Some children were reversing such letters as "p" and "g" or "b" and "d." Actually, such reversals are quite normal through second grade. The principal was interested because the children in these classrooms were beginning to doubt their own abilities. When teachers have unrealistic expectations of children, it can negatively affect self-esteem.

THE IMPORTANCE OF THE PARENT AND
SCHOOL PARTNERSHIP

How much school influences a child's self-worth depends on how much value her parents place on school experiences. If school is not very important to the family then the child's overall self-esteem will probably not be altered as much by the teacher or school. If, however, there is a strong parent and school partnership and parents highly value education, then the child's overall feelings of self-worth will be more impacted by the school.

The parental partnership with the school makes a difference in achievement as well as self-esteem. Parents of achieving children have the following traits:

1. They take a real interest in the child's school experiences.
2. They read often to their children and share stories, hobbies, games and talk with their children often.
3. They have a regular place for their child to study which is well stocked with supplies and books.
4. They monitor the amount of television watching the child does.
5. They provide structured times for meals, homework, sleep, and help the child understand these guidelines.

Further, the parents' own self-esteem is crucial to the early elementary school child's achievement and success. Parents with low self-esteem tend to display the following characteristics:

1. They try to live their lives through the child.
2. They are overly anxious about school work.
3. They see a potential problem in most things related with their children.
4. They give mixed messages about success in school.
5. They have trouble honoring their child's efforts realistically.

THE EFFECTS OF STRESS ON SELF-ESTEEM

During the preschool years hurrying children damages their self-regard. As this continues through the primary years stress can become more and more of a factor. The influence of stress is dependent on several factors. These include (1) *the child's personality,* (2) *the child's family,* (3) *the child's learning experiences,* (4) *the number of stressors,* and (5) *compensatory experiences.*

The Child's Personality

Remember back to infancy when children differ in nine temperament traits. These characteristics continue and although the environment can alter them, a child's basic personality will certainly interact with the environment. Resilient children and good students at this age tend to be better copers. Children who are more independent also tend to cope better with stress and are less susceptible to its effect on self-esteem.

The Child's Family

The child's family continues to be an important source for the child's developing self-worth. Once again, resilient children tend to develop better relationships with their parents and siblings. The parent-child interaction is bi-directional. This means the parents' decisions change the child, but the child's interactions change the parents. Stress can be increased or diminished by these interactions.

Learning Experiences

The child's learning experiences not only in school and home but in other social situations help promote or hinder feelings about self. Independent and resilient children are better at solving problems. This gives them a feeling of some control over their environment. Children with an internal locus of control tend to develop higher self-regard.

The Number of Stressors

The number of stressors in a child's life at this age will partially determine her abilities to cope and feel good about herself. For example, a child who is coping with a difficult teacher at school, the divorce of parents, a mentally ill parent, and the death of a close grandparent all at the same time will have more difficulty than the child who is dealing with only one of these stressors. Adults can help a child's self-esteem by considering the amount and number of stress factors placed on a child and do what is possible to reduce the number and effects of these stressors.

Compensatory Experiences

Sometimes the number of problems a child encounters during the primary grades is unavoidable. The death of a grandparent while the parents are going through a divorce cannot be helped. However, positive experiences can sometimes compensate or cancel out some of the negative affects. A child who has a hobby, an interest or an experience that is positive can do much. The primary grades are an important time for the development and encouragement of individuality and uniqueness.

THE CONTINUING DEVELOPMENT OF INDIVIDUALITY

A major requirement of self-worth is a feeling of uniqueness and individuality. An important time to tap into this individuality is when the child is in the early elementary grades. The uniqueness of a child can be found in (1) *types of intelligences,* (2) *learning styles,* and (3) *personality traits*.

Types of Intelligences

Dr. Howard Gardner of Harvard University suggests we have been asking the wrong questions about children. We have been asking questions like, "How smart is my child?" when we should have been asking, "How is my child smart?" He developed a theory of multiple intelligences and explains that children can be smart in one or two areas and not smart in others. A child can be good at mathematics but have little musical ability, or just the opposite. A child cannot be expected to be good at everything. The old saying, "No one is good at everything but everyone is good at something," is especially important to remember at this age. How we communicate to a child about our expectations and her abilities will build or destroy her self-regard.

To date, Dr. Gardner has described seven types of intelligences. Each type of intelligence has little to do with another type. These include (1) *musical,* (2) *visual-spatial,* (3) *bodily-kinesthetic,* (4) *mathematical-logical,* (5) *linguistic,* (6) *interpersonal,* and (7) *intrapersonal.*

The point here is we should seek out what a child enjoys and in which she excels and help her experience it fully. Children are often good at things we do not value and are not so good at things we want them to be good at. Adults need to consider the child's abilities and not the parents' own preconceived ideas about what the child's strengths should be.

Learning Styles

Another way to develop individuality is to honor children's learning styles. Some children learn better in school by listening, others by seeing, and some learn better through hands-on experiences. Some children may need phonics to help them read while others may not. Teachers may or may not consider the individual learning styles, but parents can certainly seek ways their children learn best when helping them with their homework. Valuing how children learn is just as important as appreciating what they learn.

Personality Traits

While we should value everyone's personality traits at all ages, it is especially important to understand a child's typology at this age. Specifically, a child may be an introvert or an extravert; a sensate or intuitive; a thinker or a feeler, or a perceiver or a judger. For a better understanding of these personality dimensions I recommend reading *Please Understand Me* by David Keirsey and

Marilyn Bates.

Some children are introverts; some are extraverts. Some children prefer to play alone. While children really develop true friendships during this age, we still need to respect a child's need for privacy. Every child needs some place to call her own and this space should be respected as private.

Some elementary children are sensates while others are intuitives. Some elementary children are more aware of their outside environment than others, but there are also children who have a rich inner life. Children at this age can still have a profound fantasy life if we have not yet destroyed it. For those who enjoy fantasy and "living inside their heads" more than outside, we still need to respect this quality.

Some children are thinkers; others are feelers. Accepting how children make decisions is also important. Some like to think things through when they choose a new shirt but others are more concerned with how something makes them feel. In short, some children make decisions from the head while others make decisions from the heart. However the child makes choices, her decision-making process should be valued.

Perhaps one of the most sensitive areas of self-esteem in elementary children is the amount of structure they prefer. Some children like and need much structure in their lives. These children tend to get along fairly well with parents and teachers who need structure. The problem arises when the parents have a strong need for structure and the child does not. If a parent has a high need for a structured room with a place for everything and everything in its place that is fine. However, if a child does not have a high need for structure and leaves her toys, clothes, and things around the room this does not mean she does this to make her parents angry.

Martha is a mother of seven-year-old Zach. Martha has always had a strong need for structure. She adheres to the idea of everything in its place. Zach has very little need or interest in structure. He sometimes leaves his clothes on the floor when he changes them and does not put things back where they belong. This irritates Martha who believes that Zach is irresponsible and leaves things around just to make her mad.

The issue here is not that Martha or Zach should change their personalities. However, they both have to live in the same house. Martha needs to understand that Zach does not leave things around to make his mother mad. Zach needs to realize that his mother enjoys things in their place. Martha can expect Zach to comply with her structure needs but also needs to provide him with space, if possible, that allows him his own turf in which such structure is not demanded.

SOME MORE PRACTICAL CONCRETE SUGGESTIONS FOR ENCOURAGING SELF-ESTEEM FOR CHILDREN AGES SIX THROUGH NINE

1. Help children succeed in school. Their ideas about schooling and how they succeed in school are formed during this stage.
2. Remember that children at this age are eager to please and may give up their integrity and interests to please adults, both parents and teachers. For this reason, consider with care what you ask a child to do at this age. Decide whether what is asked is your own need or in the best interest of the child.
3. Encourage children and take an interest in their schoolwork. It is during this time that children begin to develop feelings of inferiority about their schoolwork and their abilities.
4. Be careful not to expect too much or too little of the primary aged child. Self-fulfilling prophecy is very much at work. This means children are often changed by what we think of them and expect of them.
5. As with younger children, model high self-esteem and praise yourself. Above all, live your own life and do not expect

the child to live out your unfulfilled dreams.

6. Understand the influence stress has on self-esteem. You can help by showing interest in the child, providing positive learning experiences, reducing the number of stressors when possible, and creating compensatory experiences.

7. Seek out the individuality of the child. Try to find the child's types of intelligences, learning styles, personality traits, and interests.

8. Children need opportunities to choose and have some sense of power and control over their environment. Give them freedom to choose their hobbies and interests within reason. Support these and convey confidence in their ability to make wise choices, encouraging them when they do.

9. Avoid comparative practices. Do not compare the primary aged child with siblings or other children. The child who has problems needs to be compared only with herself—how much progress SHE makes—how much initiative SHE takes.

10. Help children develop ways to live within the rules of school and society. When other adults are unreasonable, communicate to the child that you know she has the ability to survive and believe in her capacity to do so.

OTHER RESOURCES TO HELP YOU FOLLOW UP WHAT YOU HAVE LEARNED IN THIS CHAPTER

Canfield, Jack, and Wells, Harold. *100 Ways to Enhance Self-concept in the Classroom.* Englewood Cliffs, NJ: Prentice Hall, 1976.
This book provides teachers and parents with many practical suggestions for helping children build their self-esteem in schools.

Clemes, Harris, and Bean, Reynold. *How to Raise Children's Self-esteem.* San Jose, CA: Enrich, 1980.
Parents can use this resource to better understand how they can help children

feel good about themselves in an authentic way.

Gardner, Howard. *Frames of Mind: The Theory of Multiple Intelligences.* New York: Basic Books, 1983.

This is a great resource explaining Dr. Gardner's views on intelligences. The book can serve as a reference for helping understand and finding methods to capitalize children's strengths.

Rosenthal, Robert, and Jacobson, Lenore. *Pygmalion in the Classroom.* New York: Holt, Rinehart and Winston, 1968.

Self-fulfilling prophecy means that children give us what we expect of them. This book reports the Oak School study mentioned in this chapter which illustrates this point.

CHAPTER FIVE

DEVELOPING SELF-ESTEEM IN PREADOLESCENCE
(NINE THROUGH TWELVE)

Preadolescence is an emerging category defined as a critical period between childhood and the teen years. Preadolescence is a sensitive time for self-esteem development. With the exception of the first years of life, more developmental experiences occur during preadolescence than at any other time of life. Decisions about self-esteem and independence are based on personal experiences which occur during this important time.

Self-esteem is vulnerable during this age group because the preadolescent is affected by three important groups. These include (1) *the family,* (2) *the school,* and (3) *informal and formal peer groups.* Self-esteem is also challenged by emerging themes of preadolescence.

As a child moves into preadolescence, parents, teachers, and other significant adults may have less influence and control over the preteen as the peer group becomes the major social contributor to self-esteem. There is also a renewed need for autonomy and sepa-rateness from adults. Just as the two year old asserts individuality, the preadolescent is assertive. This time around, though, the child is significantly influenced by other children. This group influence peaks between the ages of eleven and twelve and then begins to decline.

THE FAMILY AND SELF-ESTEEM

Even though the peer group is important to the preadolescent, the family has the major impact on beliefs and values. Preadolescents ranked having a happy family as their highest value in a survey conducted by the Search Institute. The majority of preadolescents are close to their parents, and it is within the family context most preadolescents want to discuss their problems.

An example of the continuing importance of the family is Carol. Carol is an only child and attends the public school while most of her friends at church attend a private school. Carol is often excluded from parties by her church friends because she attends a public school.

Fortunately, Carol communicates freely with her parents and discussed the dilemma with them. Both Carol and her parents are aware that most of the people who attend private school in her community do so because they believe there is a racial imbalance in the public school. To put it bluntly, they feel there are too many African Americans in the public schools.

Carol's parents listened as she described her hurt and disappointments about her exclusion from certain parties because of where she attends school. Carol has adopted her family's beliefs and values and accepts the choice of a public education as one that expresses the family's views and acceptance of other races and cultures.

By simply being good listeners and feeling Carol's pain with her, her parents are key players in helping Carol compensate for the rejection she is facing. Her parents do not "preach" to Carol, nor do they ignore her true feelings. They do not encourage Carol to "get over her pity party." They don't even try to make it all better. Carol's parents are confident in their own self-worth and decision making. Her parents serve as models of high self-regard. Carol sees this in her parents, and she is able to strengthen her own self-esteem.

THE SCHOOL

The school also contributes much to the preadolescent's developing sense of self. In a study of the relationship between academic achievement (grades), academic performance (standardized test scores), and social peer relations, Dr. Lisa Henderson found that in both third and sixth grades report card grades were highly significant to self-esteem. Although Dr. Henderson's study had limitations, she found that report card grades were even more important than peer relations.

Another way school influences self-esteem is through the changes preadolescents go through when they move from elementary school to middle or junior high school. Some studies show that a child's self-esteem drops around seventh grade—a time when many of them are entering junior high school with new demands, such as a larger school and changing classes. While teachers have less influence on self-worth during this period, instructors can prepare an environment to encourage self-regard as the preadolescent faces new demands.

THE PEER GROUP

The consequences of peer group participation are strongly related to self-concept and self-esteem. The peer group is generally the indicator of social acceptance or rejection.

Two important factors in peer group participation are *physical attractiveness* and *shared values*. Concerns about physical attractiveness increase during this period when the preadolescent is most vulnerable. Biological changes result in awkward movements and less than flattering appearances. Some preadolescents may be quick to stereotype body types with personality traits. Muscular and athletic children may be seen as strong, smart, brave, and helpful while stout children may be viewed as lazy, jolly, or sloppy. Skinny children may be seen as weak, quiet, or worrisome.

There is a major growth spurt during later preadolescence which influences self-esteem development. Typically, girls begin their growth spurt before boys. This is apparent in the changes in size of girls when compared to boys around fifth and sixth grades. These physical changes are associated with puberty. However, individual differences in terms of the age of onset of puberty can be extreme. Children may go through puberty as early as nine or as late as seventeen. Early puberty for both sexes is associated with a stout physique while later onset is more characteristic of a thin body type.

What influence does this growth spurt have on social acceptance and self-esteem? Ironically, early maturation seems to be a plus for boys. Early maturing girls tend to have more problems as well as late maturing girls.

Linda is in the fifth grade and has already gone through menarche. She is fully a foot taller than most of the boys in her classroom, and she is very aware of her early maturation. Her fast growth makes her uncomfortable and self-conscious around her peers, especially the boys.

Derrick is in the eighth grade and is shorter than most of the boys in junior high school. Most of his classmates have developed body hair and have started shaving. Derrick is later in maturing and is concerned about this. He is often teased during P. E. class. Some of the boys have made fun of his size and nicknamed him "Runt." Although Derrick has some athletic potential, his size is influencing both his social acceptance and his feelings about himself.

Shared values is also an important part of social interaction during this period. Larry is a member of a conservative religious group and his family practices the beliefs of their religion. Larry has received much grief from his peers about the foods he eats, the clothes he wears, and the differences of his religious practices.

Fortunately, Larry has made friends with peers like Carol, mentioned earlier in this chapter, who have been taught to value different races, religions, and cultures. Parents affect not only the child's value system but expectations and tolerance for others who do not share the same values. Adults should have high standards about accepting and valuing other people's rights and customs. Still, the peer group can be terribly cruel at this age for those who are not of the same social, racial, or cultural class. This can influence preadolescent minority students when they are subjected to narrow-minded or rigid attitudes of classmates.

EMERGING THEMES

Major concerns and themes emerge during preadolescence. Dr. M. Strommen, who wrote *Five Cries of Youth,* found self-esteem, family well-being, welfare of people, personal advantage, and personal faith to be areas of great interest to preadolescents and adolescents. He describes five cries of youth which include (1) *the cry of self-hatred,* (2) *the cry of psychological orphans,* (3) *the cry of social concern,* (4) *the cry of prejudice,* and (5) *the cry of the joyous.* The last three cries are especially characteristic of adolescence. However, the first two (those of self-hatred and psychological orphans) are part of the preadolescent's experience and deserve consideration here.

The Cry of Self-Hatred
Dr. Strommen contends there are few sufferings as difficult as feelings of inadequacy and worthlessness. He lists three self-relational characteristics associated with low self-esteem. These are personal faults, lack of self-confidence, and low estimate of worth.

Causes of self-hatred are both internal and external. Internal factors include personality and physical attributes. Such characteristics as introversion are not valued in the American culture. The introverted preadolescent may have difficulty relating to both adults and peers. External sources which influence self-hatred have already been described as the family, the school, and the peer group.

The Cry of Psychological Orphans

The second cry of preadolescence arises from the need for a stable home life which is supportive, accepting, and loving in which people care about one another. This need is sometimes undermined by significant changes in the family structure.

Families have changed quite a bit in the past fifty years. Divorce, parental job mobility, single parent homes, working mothers, and hurried families contribute to a preadolescent's feelings of abandonment. Psychological abandonment of the family places more responsibility on other social institutions to facilitate self-esteem, moral values, and spiritual development.

What can be done to help the preadolescent achieve a healthy self-esteem at a time when ecological factors are creating preadolescents with the cry of self-hatred and the cry of psychological orphans? Preadolescents can be taught to build their own self-esteem to a point where it is not dependent on someone else saying you are OK. Most preadolescents know when they feel good about themselves. Since preadolescents are aware of their self-esteem, they can learn ways to manage it by identifying what makes them feel good, what they do well, and how they feel when achieving success.

SOME MORE PRACTICAL CONCRETE SUGGESTIONS

There are many things which can be done to encourage self-esteem during preadolescence. Some of these include:
1. Remember that many developmental changes are going on during this time which will influence self-esteem. These include a shift of emphasis to the peer group, physical changes,

and changes in school environments (such as a move to middle or junior high school). Because of these developmental changes, be patient with the preadolescent.

2. Make sure lines of communication are open to the preadolescent. Be a good listener and available to listen to the preadolescent's dilemmas and concerns.

3. Prepare the preadolescent for body changes such as the onset of puberty. Describe these changes as normal and show confidence in the preadolescent in getting through this difficult period. Have confidence in the preteen to survive these changes.

4. Remember that school achievement is important to self-worth during this period. Understand that grades may temporarily drop but convey confidence in the child and do not indicate that acceptance and self-worth are entirely dependent upon school achievement.

5. Communicate your values to the preadolescent and model high self-esteem even when your values are challenged by others. (This serves as a model for the preteen.)

6. Do not overemphasize physical attractiveness or popularity. The cry of self-hatred may emerge when personality, physical, or social traits are not unconditionally accepted.

7. Try to walk the delicate line between the preadolescent's need for growing independence and their feeling of psychological abandonment. Accept initiatives for independence while simultaneously being there when needed.

8. Teach preadolescents to monitor their own self-esteem. This can be accomplished by taking pride in your own accomplishments when others do not and by promoting the child's acceptance of achievement and failures without being dependent on others' approval. This is most difficult during preadolescence. The best way to do this is to have a good relationship with the preadolescent (by being supportive and listening) and by modeling this behavior as much as possible.

OTHER RESOURCES TO HELP YOU FOLLOW UP WHAT YOU LEARNED IN THIS CHAPTER

Aldridge, Jerry. "Preadolescence." In Don Ratcliff & J. A. Davies (Eds.), *Handbook of Youth Ministry*. Birmingham, AL: Religious Education Press, pp. 97-118, 1991.
This is one of the few chapters ever written on this age group known as preteens or preadolescents. It describes what the preadolescent is like, what to expect, and how to help them accept themselves during this period.

Kohen-Raz, Reuven. *The Child from 9 to 13: Psychology and Psychopathology*. Chicago: Aldine-Atherton, 1971.
Although the title of this book sounds very professional, the book is easy to read and is a practical guide to understanding the preadolescent child.

Minuchin, Patricia. *The Middle Years of Childhood*. Monterey, CA: Brooks/Colet, 1977.
The middle years of childhood (including the preteen years) are described in this book with regard to physical, social, emotional, personality, and intellectual development. The book is easy to read and also provides helpful suggestions for working with preteens.

CHAPTER SIX

DEVELOPING SELF-ESTEEM IN ADOLESCENCE
(TWELVE THROUGH NINETEEN)

Most people recognize adolescence as a very stressful time. From the upheaval experienced by many adolescents you might assume that self-esteem drops during this period. However, research on adolescence shows that there may, in fact, be a slight but consistent increase in self-esteem during adolescence. Most research, though, is reported on groups of adolescents and not on individual cases. Some adolescents may individually have a dramatic shift in their self-esteem, but the norm seems to be that self-esteem remains relatively constant or increases slightly over the teen years. In this chapter, we will consider (1) *how adolescents describe themselves,* (2) *what influences the adolescents' self-esteem,* and (3) *the importance of self-esteem during the teenage years.*

HOW ADOLESCENTS DESCRIBE THEMSELVES

Adolescents have a greater capacity to describe themselves in terms of their self-concept and self-esteem. There are four levels of self-descriptions. In early childhood the self is described in a group of separate categories. There is a lack of ability in young children to describe an integrated or whole self-esteem. Children describe themselves in terms of physical characteristics or preferences. In the primary grades and preadolescence, children begin to describe themselves in relation to other people. They may describe themselves in terms of how they relate to their friends. They may say they can do this or that better or worse than their peers. The self is beginning to be talked about in reference to social settings. During early adolescence, individuals describe themselves even more in terms of social interactions. Their physical characteristics and self-appeal have now become more important. By later adolescence, people are able to talk about themselves more in terms of a philosophy of life, moral standards, or a system of beliefs. Thus, by this period, individuals have a better handle on how to describe themselves. Adolescents have a better overall view of self-esteem rather than just specific self-esteems.

There are differences in teenagers' descriptions if we look at temporary versus more permanent self-esteem. *Barometric self-esteem* is an idea in which a person fluctuates from time to time. For example, if a teen asks someone for a date and is turned down, he or she may have temporary low self-esteem. Baseline or more *permanent self-esteem* may not be affected in the long run. What tends to impact adolescents' self-esteem more than temporary setbacks are *parental influences, social class, physical appearance,* and *thinking abilities.*

PARENTS AND THE TEENAGERS' SELF-ESTEEM

Parents still have an influence on their teenager's self-esteem, although it may not seem like it. The type of parenting that most encourages self-esteem in adolescents is a democratic parenting style (as opposed to permissive at one extreme or authoritarian at the other). This is true not only for white adolescents, but also for Hispanics, Asians, and African American adolescents as well.

What can parents of teenagers do to help their children with self-esteem? The following characteristics are optimal for self-worth development. First, the parents can work to make the adolescent feel loved and wanted. Second, the parents can exercise discipline that shows concern for the welfare of the teenager and fairness in punishment. These actions make for the best possible influence parents can have on their teenagers.

Social Class and the Teenagers' Self-esteem

Social class may have something to do with self-esteem, because adolescents are more aware of this phenomenon. Teens with friends in a higher social class tend to have higher self-esteem. Adolescents are more conscious of social status, and it may or may not influence their feelings about themselves.

Physical Appearance and Teenagers' Self-esteem

In the chapter on preadolescence, we looked at the impact of early and late maturing on self-esteem. Physical attractiveness is also extremely important in adolescence. Some studies show that physical appearance may be the single most important component of global self-esteem for teenagers. This may be even more true for females than males because females report more problems adjusting to the physical changes of this developmental period.

Thinking Abilities and Teenagers' Self-esteem

As was mentioned earlier, adolescents increasingly describe themselves in abstract terms. This is partly due to increased thinking abilities. The ability to think about the self is still tied to school performance and test scores. Adolescents with higher self-esteem tend to do better in school and perform higher on standardized tests. This is the old chicken-and-egg dilemma, of which came first. Do adolescents do better in school because they have high self-esteem, or do they have high self-esteem because they are doing so well in school?

THE IMPORTANCE OF SELF-ESTEEM

Self-concept and self-esteem are important during adolescence for many reasons. The major reason that it is important is the relationship of self-esteem to *general adjustment, vocational choice,* and *delinquency*.

Feelings of Self-worth and Adjustment

Self-esteem in adolescents is directly related to healthy adjustment. The flip side of this is that low self-esteem during this time is related to unhealthy emotional development, vulnerability to criticism and rejection, avoidance of social situations, depression, and, sometimes, even suicide.

Adolescents with low self-esteem are more likely to be nervous and demonstrate psychosomatic illnesses according to developmental psychologist Dr. Susan Harter. They tend to be more worried about being sick and more often demonstrate insomnia. Adolescents with higher self-esteem are less likely to demonstrate or develop these symptoms.

Also, teenagers with low self-regard are more sensitive to criticism and worry more about being rejected by others. They are often more concerned about their looks and mannerisms than teens who feel more self-confident. Adolescents who feel good about themselves worry less about criticism and rejection and are better adjusted socially.

Teens with low self-esteem often avoid social situations because of this fear of rejection. They often feel awkward around others and expect to fail in their social relations. This feeling of insecurity is picked up by their peers and a vicious cycle of rejection and fear is formed. Teenagers with higher self-esteem feel confident, and this confidence puts others at ease. They develop a cycle of confidence which promotes ease among their peers, which, in turn, gives them more confidence in social situations.

Self-esteem is also related to depression in teenagers. Those with low self-regard tend not to do as well in school or situations that please their parents and peers. Because of this, they may develop a sense of helplessness and feel that anything they do will be wrong. This causes feelings of depression and lack of involvement. Teens with high self-worth feel that they have more control over their environment. They believe that their actions can be pleasing to themselves and others and that they can make a difference in their own happiness as well as the happiness of others.

Feelings of helplessness and depression are indicative of suicidal tendencies during these years. *Low self-esteem is not the only contributor to suicidal tendencies, but it is certainly a major factor. Conversely, teens who feel they have some control over their world and feel good about their worth are less likely to contemplate suicide.*

Self-esteem and Vocational Choice

Self-esteem directly affects an adolescent's thoughts and decisions about a future career. Adolescents with poor self-esteem seem to take one of two options. Either they may have lower vocational expectations, or they may choose a career to please their parents or others. Even if this career is admirable (such as a physician or lawyer), it may not be what the teenager would have chosen for himself or herself.

Joan is a very smart seventeen-year-old but does not feel good about her academic abilities. She would like to go to medical school but has a great fear that she would not succeed. Consequently, she is considering medical technology because she feels she would have a better chance of succeeding. There is nothing wrong with a career in medical technology. Many bright and confident adolescents consider this career. The problem is, it is really Joan's second choice because of her feelings of inferiority and inadequacy.

Joan's classmate Don, on the other hand, is considering medical school, not because he wants to, but because his parents would like to have a physician in the family. Don is much more interested in theater and drama and has fantasies about becoming an actor. However, he puts this on the back burner because of what people might think. After all, his parents want him to be a doctor, and he wants to please them. A close look at this situation shows he is much like Joan—they both have a low sense of self-regard. In Joan's case, she fears failure. In Don's case, he fears parental disapproval. The main difference is that Joan's decision is based on internal doubts, while Don's decision is based on external pressures. They will both be unhappy if they do not attempt to follow their hearts and go with their first love.

Self-esteem and Juvenile Delinquency

The causes of juvenile delinquency are many, and deciding what causes it is often difficult. However one thing is relatively certain—*teens who are delinquent have low feelings of self-worth*. The self-esteem mirror is at work in juvenile delinquents. They see themselves in the way that others see them. They have little respect for themselves because others look at them as bad, ignorant, or lazy and juvenile delinquents tend to agree with the evaluation others place on them.

Most of the variables which contribute to delinquency are related in some ways to self-esteem development. The parents' or guardians' child-rearing style and rejection, later reinforced by teachers and peers, provide the impetus for living out delinquent behavior. *Teenagers, more than any other age group, live out what others see them to be, which reinforces the way they see themselves*. If we expect an adolescent to be delinquent, chances are our expectations will be realized.

SOME MORE CONCRETE PRACTICAL SUGGESTIONS FOR WORKING WITH TEENAGERS' SELF-ESTEEM

1. Accept the fact that teenagers are better able to communicate their own ideas and listen to their viewpoints even when it differs from your own.

2. Involve the adolescent in family decision making. Remember, the democratic parenting style is more promoting of self-esteem than the authoritarian or permissive.

3. Accept the adolescent's cry for individuality and identity. Understand that taste in clothing, hair, music, and other items of interest may go through a bizarre period during which the adolescent is experimenting with individuality and identity.

4. Be very sensitive to the adolescent's feelings of attractiveness. Physical appearance may be the most contributing factor toward total self-esteem during this period.

5. Respect an adolescent's idealism and interest in a career. Above all, do not suggest a teenager choose a career which is pleasing to you. Respect their interests and views with regard to vocational choices.

6. After respecting a teenager's vocational views, find out what he or she really wants to do. Since some adolescents under-shoot their visions because of a lack of self-worth, ask them, "What would you really like to do?" and encourage them to go after their vision if at all possible.

7. Respect the privacy of a teenager. Allow self-expressions through room decoration and respect sentimental or peculiar possessions that he or she sees as valuable.

8. Allow the adolescent autonomy to perform duties the way he or she chooses. Teenagers need opportunities to explore their new thinking and problem-solving abilities to enhance their feelings of competency.

9. Accept the changing role of a teenager. The adolescent is now first and foremost a member of the peer group, and family participation may be less important to them.

10. Discuss family rules and have a clear channel for communication. Spell out how grievances are handled within the family.

11. Be a good model of problem solving for teenagers and intro-

duce them to others who can serve as exemplary role models. This can be done through personal contacts or through literature.

12. Be alert to signs of depression and lack of social interaction. Encourage the teen to communicate exasperation and feelings.

13. Most of all, believe in the teenager and in your ability to get through difficult times. Have faith in yourself and have faith in your adolescent.

Remember, *adolescents are much better able to use their minds and have choices about self-esteem*. For this reason, I have included a list of things adolescents can do to monitor and maintain their own sense of self-worth.

FURTHER SUGGESTIONS FOR ADOLESCENTS TO IMPROVE THEIR OWN SELF-ESTEEM

1. Believe in yourself, even when nobody else does.

2. Find out what you really like to do and go for it. If it's cheerleading and you don't make the team, find another constructive outlet and source of enjoyment.

3. Remember, looks are not everything. It's what's inside that counts, and it's what's inside that you can make beautiful.

4. Remember what Eleanor Roosevelt said, "No one can make you feel bad without your consent."

5. It's important to know that when other teens make fun of you because of your physical appearance, the way you dress, or your abilities, they are usually insecure themselves. As a child you may have knocked over a vase and told your mom that someone else did it. Ironically, that's what criticizers are doing to you. They are, in effect, saying, "Look at how ugly he or she is—don't look at me" (because I'm ugly).

6. Stick to your ground about what you want to do with a career

when you know what you want to do and you know you're right. If you want to be an artist, but your parents want you to be an engineer, tell them how much you want to be an artist. In the long run, you'll be happier, and they will too!

OTHER RESOURCES TO HELP YOU FOLLOW UP WHAT YOU LEARNED IN THIS CHAPTER

Clark, Aminah, Clemes, Harris and Bean, Reynold. *How to Raise Teenagers' Self-esteem.* San Jose, CA: Enrich, 1980.

This resource was written for parents and teachers who want to learn ways to provide connectiveness, uniqueness, power, and good models for teenagers. A special section is written about conditions of self-esteem in the family. Practical suggestions are given on determining a program to enhance adolescents' self-esteem and how to deal with your own negative feelings.

Dusek, Jerome. *Adolescent Development and Behavior* (2nd ed.). Englewood Cliffs, NJ: Prentice Hall, 1991.

This comprehensive guide describes every aspect of adolescent life from social development to juvenile delinquency, from intellectual development to mental problems. There is a special section on self-esteem which reports research and findings on adolescent self-esteem development.

Muuss, Rolf. *Adolescent Behavior and Society: A Book of Readings* (3rd ed.). New York: Random House, 1980.

Social development in adolescence profoundly affects self-esteem development. This book of readings emphasizes the social development of teenagers, and it incorporates how this influences adolescent self-worth.

CHAPTER SEVEN

DEVELOPING SELF-ESTEEM IN EARLY ADULTHOOD
(TWENTY THROUGH THIRTY-FIVE)

Early adulthood may be defined as ages twenty through thirty-five. The ages of early adulthood vary from person to person, but we will consider self-esteem development in early adulthood to be within this range.

Personality development does not stop when a person stops physically growing—far from it. Personality develops throughout life, and self-esteem remains a continuing theme through the lifespan. What do most adults base their self-esteem around? Two broad areas seem to consume much early adulthood—**love** and **work**.

SELF-ESTEEM AND LOVE

Loving someone else involves self-worth first. In order to be intimate with someone else, a person must first like themselves. Just what, though, is meant by love. To answer this, it is helpful to consider internationally known psychologist Dr. Robert J. Sternberg's triangular theory of love. According to Dr. Sternberg, love has three different faces: *intimacy, passion,* and *commitment*.

Intimacy is self-disclosure which is related to trust, connectedness, and warmth. Passion usually involves sexual desire based on physiological drives. Commitment is the thinking part of love. It is the conscious decision to love someone and stick with them for better or worse.

Love in early adulthood often involves marriage. A good marriage tends to promote self-worth. In a study of approximately two-thousand adults in the United States, the happiest people were those who were married in their twenties, but had no children. However, this trend seems to be changing. People who have never married are happier today, while people who are married seem less happy. Today, sex and intimacy are more accessible outside of marriage, and people are learning that marriage is not a prerequisite for feeling fulfilled and complete.

With regard to self-esteem, marriage can enhance feelings of self-worth only if these feelings are present to begin with. People make a big mistake when they marry someone to fulfill their self-worth needs. A person can only reflect back what is already there. By early adulthood, each person is definitely responsible for his or her own self-esteem.

This is supported by what makes a successful marriage. What does make a successful marriage? Part of the answer can be found in the way partners communicate and confront conflict. This, again, involves self-esteem. Showing anger or arguing can actually be good for a marriage, whereas whining, stubbornness, and defensiveness can destroy it. Couples who communicate and confront problems have more successful marriages. People with high self-esteem are better at confronting problems, showing anger, and expressing their true feelings, which, in turn, builds the marriage.

Violence and abuse in marriage are also associated with self-esteem—low self-esteem. Men who are abusive to their wives tend to have low self-worth, be jealous and socially isolated, and often blame their wives for their own problems. Why do women stay with men who abuse them? The answer, again, is low self-esteem.

They may feel so bad about themselves that they believe they deserve to be abused.

Young adults may be married, divorced, single, or even widowed, yet within each category are people who feel good about themselves and people who do not. So, what makes the difference? Happiness and the ability to love and accept love are all dependent on self-concept and self-esteem. A person must love self before being able to give love or accept love from another. Obviously, it is not the marital category that enables a person to give and receive love in early adulthood. The choice to love oneself first is what makes the difference.

SELF-ESTEEM AND WORK

The choice of a career is also made based in part on self-esteem. In the chapter on adolescence we have already seen two mistakes made by people with low self-worth. One was choosing a career to match one's low expectations. The other error was choosing an admirable or prestigious profession to please one's parents or spouse.

The choice of a career is not solely a rational choice. There are many factors involved, some of which include parental pressures, socioeconomic status, race, ethnicity, and encouragement from teachers or peers. All of these influences impact on an individual's sense of self. People with the highest sense of self choose a career based on what they enjoy. People who do not have a high sense of self choose careers based on what other people expect of them. Authentic career choice involves the highest self-regard. Career choice always tests a person's true feelings.

What makes for success in the job during early adulthood? Charles Garfield of the Peak Performance Center in Berkeley, California studied 1500 individuals from all walks of life and discovered seven keys to success. It was not luck, connections, or even hard work that made for success, but other factors—factors which we can all learn. All seven of these traits, though, are also associated with high self-esteem. Successful individuals (1) *have a well-rounded life,* (2) *choose careers they care about,* (3) *work hard but are not perfectionists,* (4) *are willing to take risks,* (5) *do not underestimate their abilities,* (6) *compete with themselves but not others,* and (7) g*o over difficult tasks in their minds before performing them.*

Having a Well-Rounded Life

A well-rounded life is often difficult to achieve in early adulthood. Young adults who are consumed with school, starting a career, and developing a marriage find it hard to concentrate on these, much less to find time for anything else. The high price paid for this one-sided life catches up with us in middle adulthood.

Successful people with high self-esteem do not spend all of their time at work. They learn early in adulthood to maintain a certain balance between work and play, family and hobbies, and group and individual pursuits. Dr. Garfield found that successful people who like themselves know how to relax. They do not spend all of their time at work or the office. They find time for friends and family life and spend a great deal of time with their spouses and children.

Choosing a Career You Care About

In the past thirty years, more people have been choosing careers based on the amount of money they will earn as opposed to careers they would enjoy. Those with high self-esteem choose careers they care about and jobs they enjoy. When such choices are made, high financial rewards often follow. Even if they don't, the personal rewards outweigh any amount of money earned in a job that is unsatisfying.

Working Hard but not Being a Perfectionist

People who are successful work hard, but they are not perfectionists. The artist or writer who waits for the perfect product is both unrealistic and less productive. Take, for example, someone who is writing a book on the uses of computers. If this person waits until the book is "perfect," it will be out of date, because so many other uses of computers will have been developed while the book was being perfected. Adults with high self-esteem acknowledge humanness and accept the fact that they are not perfect and never will be.

The Willingness to Take Risks

It is well known that successful adults with high self-esteem experience more failures than unsuccessful people do with low self-worth. Now how is this possible? One example of this phenomenon is Mem Fox, the famous Australian writer of children's books. She submitted her first book eight times before it was finally accepted for publication. What if she had only sent it out five or six times? She was willing to take risks and accept rejection in her pursuit of success. She faced more failures than someone who sent out a manuscript only a few times and gave up, but, because Ms. Fox was persistent and willing to take risks, she has achieved a successful career.

Estimating Your Own Abilities

Successful people do not underestimate their potential. As mentioned in the previous chapter, during adolescence some individuals underestimate their abilities and choose careers that are less interesting to them out of fears of failure in a more challenging profession. The ability to take risks and then go for what you want (by not underestimating your capabilities) requires true feelings of self-regard.

Competing with Yourself

People with high self-worth compete with themselves—not others. When we compare ourselves with others there will always be some who we perceive as better than us and others who are not. Feelings of centeredness and confidence in one's ability to improve self are characteristics of successful adults.

Going Over or Rehearsing Difficult Tasks

When faced with challenging situations, successful adults think over how they will deal with them before going into action. Before giving a speech, playing a recital, or accepting an award, those who are achievers rehearse until they feel confident in their ability to carry out the task. Successful people anticipate the possibilities of what might happen and prepare themselves in advance to deal with them. They actually minimize their risks by thinking things through.

SOME MORE PRACTICAL CONCRETE SUGGESTIONS

1. Develop the attitude that, as an adult, you are responsible for your own self-esteem.
2. Accept the fact that relationships, especially marriage, reflect your true feelings about yourself. You cannot expect someone else to value you if you do not like yourself. People give back to you what you show them about yourself.
3. Above all, love yourself and work toward fulfilling your own dreams. Do not expect your spouse or children to live your own unlived life—they have their own lives. Take care of your own needs so that you can better love and nurture your relationships.
4. Make a commitment to having a good relationship with yourself, since authentic, quality relationships are built upon high self-esteem. My grandfather made a habit of practicing this. He would say, "I like to talk to myself for two reasons: First, I like to talk with someone interesting; second, I like to talk to someone who is interested in the same things that I am."
5. Do not base your self-esteem on your marital status. Whether single, married, divorced, widowed, or cohabitating, your self-esteem can be either high or low. This is dependent on you, and not the other person.
6. Avoid being verbally or physically abusive to yourself or others. Abuse is indicative of low self-worth. In order to build

self-esteem, do not be abusive and refuse to accept it from others. Remember, you get what you expect.

7. Follow the seven recommendations for peak performance discovered by the Charles Garfield study.

8. Develop a career you care about and go after the type of job you want. Career choice is related to success and self-esteem. Young adults, especially males, tend to define themselves in terms of their work. Their self-esteem is often dependent upon how they feel about their work.

OTHER RESOURCES TO HELP YOU FOLLOW UP WHAT YOU LEARNED IN THIS CHAPTER

Brandon, Nathaniel. *How to Raise Your Self-esteem*. New York: Bantam Books, 1987.

Dr. Brandon has written many books about self-esteem. This one gives specific behaviors and activities you can try to build your self-esteem, particularly during early adulthood.

Brandon, Nathaniel. *The Psychology of Self-esteem*. New York: Bantam Books, 1969.

Dr. Brandon describes how self-esteem develops—particularly during the adulthood years. I suggest reading this book first, before reading *How to Raise Your Self-esteem* so that you will have a better understanding of what self-esteem is all about during the adult years. Then you will have a better idea of how to raise it.

Hunt, M. "Seven secrets of peak performance." *Reader's Digest*, September, 1982.

In this short four-page article Mr. Hunt reports and explains Dr. Charles Garfield's work which was introduced in this chapter. The article has good examples of how to reach your peak performance, especially during early adulthood.

May, Rollo. *The Courage to Create*. New York: Bantam Books, 1975.

World famous psychologist Dr. Rollo May shows the interrelatedness of self-esteem and creativity. Although Dr. May has written many scholarly and professional books, this one is a must for the young adult who wants to better understand himself or herself and the creative process which lies within all of us.

Chapter Eight

DEVELOPING SELF-ESTEEM IN MIDDLE ADULTHOOD
(THIRTY-FIVE TO SIXTY)

Self-esteem is a major issue during the mid-life years. Whether a person is successful or not is not the only determining factor of self-esteem development during this time of life. What makes self-esteem so important during middle adulthood? Why do people stop to consider their personal worth at this period of their lives? Some of the reasons include (1) *the need for a balanced life,* (2) *the onset of midlife crisis or menopause,* (3) *the recognition of our dark side of life,* and (4) *a search for the meaning of life*. All of these issues approach us from one angle or another.

THE NEED FOR A BALANCED LIFE

Up until midlife, most of our time has been spent developing a career, establishing intimacy, and doing our part to become a contributing—or at least surviving—member of society. Our efforts have been predominantly outward by necessity. We have been concerned with establishing our place in life, and most of us have had little time to develop an inner life. This eventually creates a lack of balance in our lives. Then, in midlife our focus begins to shift from outward concerns to some inner questions. One of the questions which arises is "What is this life all about?" We are forced to acknowledge a need for something more—something seems missing and we are not sure exactly what that something is.

What is it that makes us realize that something is missing? What is it that lets us know our lives are out of balance? Is it success? Is it failure? The answer to this is—both. Some people say the only thing worse in midlife than failure is success. One of the world's leading authorities on self-esteem, Dr. Bernie Siegel tells us in his book *Love, Medicine and Miracles* that we should watch out for climbing a ladder of success. If we're not careful we will reach the top and realize the ladder is leaning against the wrong wall!

By our mid-thirties, we start to become conscious of this imbalance. An imbalanced life is always expressed in an individual or unique way. Some people need to finally grow up; others have the opposite problem—they need to liven up. All of us eventually find ourselves in a tension of opposites, and discover that this is an uncomfortable place to be.

One example of this is the tension felt between the child and adult in all of us. Some psychologists use fancy words for this. The adult male who remains a child they call a ***puer***. The grown-up female who stays a child they call a ***puella***. I like to refer to them as Uncle Puer and Aunt Puella. We all know them—those people who don't want to grow up. There are endless books written about them, such as Dr. Marie Louise Von Franz's *Puer Aeternus* or Dr. Dan Kiley's *The Peter Pan Syndrome*. Puers and puellas are free-spirited, spontaneous, creative, child-like individuals who are the life of the party. We all enjoy being around them for their spontaneity and creativity. The problem with them is their lack of responsibility. They are living on one side of life—the child side. They are like Peter Pan who said, "I don't want to grow up."

The opposite extreme is the ***senex***. This is just a fancy term for the old person in all of us. Senexes are grounded in responsibility.

If they say they will do something, you can count on them. And we all count on them to get things done, for the one thing we know about them is, "They are responsible." The problem with senexes is that they don't know how to have fun—they lack spontaneity and creativity: they are too focused on work and stability.

There is a puer or puella in all of us, just as there is a senex. In midlife, we are thrown into the dilemma of how to balance these two without destroying one or the other. How can we be creative and spontaneous without being irresponsible? How can we be responsible without being boring or stuffy?

One thing we can do is identify which type of individual we seem to be more like—the puer/puella or the senex. Actually, if we are paying attention to what is happening to us we can see patterns and identify an imbalance. One profound example is Marilyn. Marilyn is a forty-year-old housewife who has gone back to college in midlife. She took a human development course under me. During this course I talked about the balance in midlife between the puer and the senex. After the course was over, I received the following letter from Marilyn.

Dear Dr. Aldridge:

I thought you might appreciate my sharing with you a profound experience I have had which, in part, came to me through participating in your Human Development course this term. Education is not just what we get from books, I've discovered. It only begins when we leave the classroom.

Since you read my life review, you know that I was the oldest of three children growing up in an alcoholic home. I was the responsible one and still am today.

About a month ago, my husband and I went to see "Hook." I discovered a part of myself in Robin Williams' character. I am, as you brought out in class, the classic example of a Senex. I am totally grounded in adulthood. When I saw Hook, I realized this about myself. When you mentioned the term, it reinforced this in my mind, but I didn't know how to deal with it.

The night of our final examination, I had a dream which brings me to what I wanted to share with you. I have had dreams before which affected me but never had the impact of this one.

I dreamed that we had gone to the funeral home because we had lost a child, a little girl. But the problem came when the little girl refused to die. She arose out of the casket and wanted to go home with us. The funeral director assured us that this sometimes happens but that she really was dead. It was just a physiological thing and would work itself out. (Weird, huh.) and that we weren't really seeing our little girl. She was just a shell (interesting). He told us that we could take the little girl home until she came to grips with the fact that she really was dead and warned us not to hold her too much or pay too much attention to her because she was "toxic" to us and didn't really belong here.

Well, I didn't know what to do with her. I put her outside. She was so cute and continued to look in from my back deck, all the while smiling and never causing a fuss. Every time I would look out, there she was.

In the middle of trying to figure out what to do with her, two men came to our door, trying to sell us a car engine. They spread out four models on our livingroom rug. My husband wanted to pay full price and I (being ever so responsible) tried to talk to them about reducing the price.

In the middle of this, I was cooking breakfast and late for a dentist appointment. In the meantime, the little girl wandered off. I was kind of glad that I didn't have to deal with her right then and wasn't worried. But my husband and children went off in search of her and found her wandering around in the woods and brought her back to the back deck, still smiling and content to just sit outside my door.

I told them that I couldn't deal with her, that they were just going to have to take her back to the funeral home themselves. I was too busy and anyway, it wasn't working—she didn't want to die.

Then I woke up. At first, I thought what a weird dream, but as I started analyzing it I realized that little girl who wouldn't go away was me. She was the Peter Pan inside me that I repressed years ago because circumstances dictated that I grow up before my time.

With all my intellectualizing about my past, I think I have reached a point where I can accommodate the little girl inside me who refused to die. I need to welcome her with open arms and do more "kid" things with her, my children, and my husband.

Thanks for your part in bringing this to the forefront of my consciousness.

Sincerely,

Marilyn

This is just one example of the many tensions that throw our self-esteem into a flux during our thirties, forties, and fifties. *So, how can we work on balancing our lives to improve our sense of self-worth?*

There are several suggestions which can be made to build a more balanced life. Just a few examples include:

1. Identify where you are spending all of your time and energy. Then try to find its opposite. If you are spending all of your time at work, what are you neglecting? Family? Leisure time activities?

2. Then, ask yourself why you are spending so much energy in one area? Is it because you are unhappy in another area? Is it because you are in a rut and can't seem to get out? Why do you think your life is out of balance?

3. Pay attention to what happens to you both **outside** *and* **inside**. Like Marilyn, you can pay attention to your interactions at work or school and you can pay attention to your dreams or fantasies. What is all of this telling you?

4. You can also talk to a friend about this or seek the help of a counselor if necessary.
5. Then, like Marilyn, make a conscious effort to try to balance what you have found is OUT of balance.

When we see that our lives are out of balance, a midlife crisis may occur. This crisis takes many forms and almost always affects our self-esteem.

MIDLIFE CRISIS AND SELF-WORTH

The way we defined our self-esteem during early adulthood and the values we developed in early life determine the themes we will face during a midlife crisis. If we based a large part of our self-esteem on *physical attractiveness*, concerns about our appearance will beset us. If we identified our personal value mostly with *our careers*, job issues will be our concern. If we focused on having a good *marriage*, marital problems will arise. If we are really concerned about all three, we will often worry about all three. In midlife we will come to question how we have constructed our worlds.

Even if we are able to cope with the physical changes of aging, job dissatisfaction, or marital strife, midlife **still** produces tension for our self-esteem. These are the "in-between" years. No other age group must live in the tension of the present like the midlifer. Youth can look forward to what life may bring and the older adults may reflect upon an exciting (or dull) life, but the command generation must live in the present. This may be due to having to shoulder responsibility for children or adolescents while also dealing with aging parents. We are the "in charge" group during this time, and it may tax our ability to cope and feel we are worthwhile.

Most men go through some midlife trauma between the ages of thirty-five and forty-five. For women, the ages are more difficult to map, due to varying timing of life changes, such as menopause or the adjustment to the empty nest. Still, most midlifers experience a crisis because of *physical aging, job considerations,* or *family issues*.

Physical Attractiveness

Something happens to our bodies in midlife that we don't like. Particularly in the United States, youth is revered, and we fear aging when we look into the mirror and see crow's feet, baldness, beer bellies, or gray hairs. A friend of mine once remarked that after forty, it's all just maintenance.

Adults who have based their self-worth on looks become quite concerned with this aging process. They may dye their hair, buy a sports car, look for a younger companion, have a facelift, and generally go off the deep end trying to maintain their youthful image. This is the time when many couples divorce. If midlife crisis were better understood, perhaps it would be easier to remain committed to a spouse and support them during this unstable time of trying to recapture youth.

Self-esteem based on appearance has to be altered unless we want to live in the past. If we are lucky, we live a rich, full life right into old age, but this is not possible for those who try to bolster their self-esteem by living in the past.

Examples of midlifers living in the past are endless. Herbert, a corporate executive officer, was a track star in high school and the pole-vault champion while in college. Now, Herbert is so fat that he cannot even bend over to tie his shoes. When his staff visits his office, Herbert shows them pictures of himself back in high school. He pulls out an old college annual that shows him doing the pole-vault. Herbert is a smart man, but his work has become dull to him and he is unproductive and uninteresting. His colleagues say that all he talks about are the good old days. Herbert put his life and self-esteem in park twenty years ago and has not made a satisfying midlife transition.

Martha has a similar problem. Although she has a successful practice as a pediatrician, she still lives in the past. She was the high school homecoming queen and head cheerleader. She is now fifty-five years old but somehow left her self-image behind and does not live in the present.

If Herbert and Martha were both ninety-five years old and retired, then their dwelling on the past would be understandable. However, they have both frozen their self-images as youths and then left themselves there—not adjusting to their changing bodies over time.

Career Adjustment in Midlife

By the middle years, people are somewhere on the career continuum—from a low point of stagnation, to a frenzied, treadmill, fast-paced upward mobility. Wherever we find ourselves on the career ladder, changes over time make us consider just what it is we are doing with our lives professionally and why we are where we are. Those people who chose their career for the prestige or to please parents or spouses are in trouble by now. They often ask, "What have I done?"

The fascinating thing about choosing a career for someone else is that it makes no one happy. Even if our parents are still proud that we are corporate executives, lawyers, or physicians, we will resent our jobs if we have not followed our true calling.

Careers are sacred, and we are drawn to them if we have followed our inner voice. If we have followed someone else's voice, by this time we realize that we are in trouble. My father, a minister, speaks often of how he was called into the ministry. I believe him and feel just as "called" and complete in my profession. Although teaching will not make me wealthy, I am rich in many ways because I am doing what I am supposed to do. I have a suspicion that my father had a secret desire for me to also be a minister. That, however, would have been a disaster. He sees how happy I am in my chosen field, and this makes him happy. Remember, as adults we are all responsible for our own self-worth and happiness. If we are true to ourselves in our careers, we may help spread some of this happiness around.

Family Issues in Midlife

There eventually comes a time in middle adulthood when we "pay the piper" for our choice of a spouse. If we married for someone else's happiness, we find that this has not been achieved. It seems all people concerned are unhappy as well.

Carl is thirty-five years old and a successful insurance salesman. He has always been a dutiful son and a "good boy," wanting to please everyone. Carl married the woman his parents wanted him to marry. He had been in love with someone else but did not marry her because she was of a different social class and religion. He figured that if he married the girl of whom his parents approved, he could make them and his wife happy, even if he would not be that happy himself.

Life does not work in this way. Carl was unhappy, even though he was trying real hard. His wife was unhappy, because she knew at some level that Carl didn't really love her. Their marital strife caused their parents concern as well. Carl and his wife had a son, and he came to share in the general unhappiness. Now Carl, being a good son, husband, and father, kept trying, but the harder he tried, the worse his family life became. His original lack of authenticity had made him miserable. Try as he would, he just couldn't make his family life work.

Finally, Carl said, "enough is enough." He divorced his wife in midlife and married the woman he had loved in his youth. For several months his family was even more unhappy than before, but eventually they accepted the situation. Now, three generations are better off because Carl followed his heart. This is what he should have done in the first place. Not all situations turn out this lucky. However, if everyone else had remained unhappy, at least Carl would have been happy, because he had finally followed his heart.

*** * ***

Midlife crisis is rough. It usually manifests itself in concerns about *physical attractiveness, work,* or *intimate relationships*. The question is, how can someone go through a midlife crisis and maintain and build self-esteem? Some practical suggestions for this include:

1. Maintain your health through exercise and diet while accepting the physical changes associated with aging.

2. Choose a career that is satisfying and in some way reflects what you want to do with your life. If you have climbed the corporate ladder in a field you do not enjoy, change careers. Most adults change careers about one or two times during their lifetime. This is a good time to consider getting into what you really want to do. (And, by the way, this takes a tremendous amount of confidence and self-esteem.)

3. Work on intimacy within yourself and with others. A sense of relatedness and relationship can blossom in midlife if you deal with your own problems and accept others as they try to work through their midlife crisis too!

DEALING WITH THE DARK SIDE OF LIFE

Our search for self-esteem is not complete in midlife if we have not considered the parts of our personality that we do not like. This is often referred to as the shadow or the dark side of life. Our dark side balanced out our masks or what we show to the outside world. The brighter our mask is, the muddier our dark side will be! It is in midlife that we face our dark side if we are truly interested in real self-esteem.

What is this dark side? Dr. Robert Bly, the famous poet and psychoanalyst, explains it well. He says that when we are born we were a whole person. Soon our parents did not like certain things about us, so we placed those things in an imaginary bag. Parents say things like, "Good boys and girls do not hit their brothers and sisters," or, "Big boys don't cry." When we entered school our teachers said, "Nice children don't talk back to the teacher or tell them what they would like to do." Then our peers began to tell us what *they* didn't like about us. We continued to stuff things into our dark-side bag, and by the time we were adults there was not much of our real personalities left out in the open. A lot of our true feelings were carefully concealed.

What is the dark side? What is in the bag? Our dark side is full of things we do not like about ourselves. Is it all bad? No. For example, as a preacher's child, I was taught that being assertive is bad. Nice boys are not assertive. However, it is necessary at times and even important to be assertive. Because it is part of my dark side, every time I am assertive, I feel guilty, even when it is appropriate.

All sorts of things go into our dark side. Perhaps you were taught that "Nice people don't enjoy sex," or, "Good people do not ask for what they want out of life." By the time we reach middle age, we are dragging so much of our dark side around, we don't know who we are or what we want.

What do we do with our dark side of life? If we do not like ourselves we most often project it onto someone else. We despise what we see in other people. The sad thing is that we are not even aware of it. If we want to be the center of attraction (but nice people are humble and are not the life of the party), we are outraged by people who insist on being the center of attention. Or, if we would like to be frivolous with our money (but nice people are frugal), then those who are spendthrifts irritate us highly.

Our dark side provides a mirror of ourselves. What we don't like about others is often the shadow within us that we do not like. There is no better mirror of our dark side in midlife than what we do not like (and feel strongly about) in others.

When television evangelists were asked what they thought about Jim Bakker's indiscretions one of the most vocal was Jimmy Swaggart. Jim Bakker was mirroring Jimmy Swaggart's dark side, and Mr. Swaggart didn't like it. But we must not be too quick to judge Mr. Swaggart. If we are consumed with disdain over his actions, it's probably because he is mirroring our own shadows.

Projecting our dark side is not the best way to deal with it—it is the coward's way out.

The only way to ever have true self-esteem and value who we are in midlife is to accept our own dark sides and stop projecting them onto other people. Doing this is very hard, because our dark side likes to hide and deceive us. Our mirrors are distorted when we deal with the shadow. It is hard to look at shadows and see them for what they are.

Sometimes we have to search for what our dark sides are really telling us. For example, I have a friend who is a highly successful, respected member of the community. Yet she seeks emotional support and companionship from her dog, rather than risk the painful aspects of human companionship. She rarely dates for fear of rejection. She does not fear rejection from her dog and often talks of the unconditional love her dog provides. This is highly upsetting to me.

Now, I don't have a dog, so at first glance I could assume that this has nothing to do with my dark side. But I need to look again. I have a strong emotional reaction to this woman's relationship to her dog. The mirror is telling me that I am depending on something else besides human companionship for my own emotional needs. Since I do not have a pet, what could it be?

Recently, I was in a situation with good friends who were discussing intimate and painful aspects of their lives. All I wanted to do was slip outside and smoke a cigarette, which I did. There it was. I depend on cigarettes to give me my emotional security. Think of how much worse this is than a dog. At least the dog is not a risk for cancer or heart disease.

Others provide an important mirror for our shadows. They tell us much about our true feelings, but sometimes we have to look deep into the mirror to discover what it is we do not like about ourselves. It was very difficult for me to look beyond the dog and find the cigarettes!

What does our dark side have to do with our self-esteem? The answer in midlife is, *everything*. In order to truly love ourselves, we must take ownership of our own dark side and not make others carry it around for us. We all have a heavy bag to deal with, and we cannot expect others to carry it for us. We find that we have asked a spouse or child or parent to deal with our own trash. The dark side is ours, and, by owning it, we can learn to accept ourselves, which is an important step before we can accept and value others for who they really are.

The following are a few suggestions for dealing with your shadow to improve your self-esteem:

1. Look closely at people you really do not like. What about them upsets you? Work hard to determine this to identify what you do not like about yourself.
2. Then, look for something good which could come out of your dark side. Often a creative spirit is found deep within our dark side.
3. Put your dark side to work for you. If you detest people who are too rigid, release the person who is too rigid within you. How? By being creative. Do something which is constructive but not usually characteristic of you. For example, if you hate spontaneous people, be spontaneous yourself in a positive way. Take time out to go and visit a nursing home or volunteer your time—spontaneously.

There is a creative gem deep within your dark side. Try to find it and use it. It will make for a more balanced life and free you to be more authentic.

THE SEARCH FOR PURPOSE

The world-renowned psychologist Dr. Carl Jung believed that we cannot stand a meaningless life. I would add, we cannot stand a purposeless life. We can attach meaning to anything. We can look back at our homecoming program from high school and attach the meaningfulness of fond memories. Meaning is not so much the issue as purpose. Barbara J. Braham in her book *Finding Your Purpose* says that meaning is the importance we attach to something. Purpose, however, is quite different. We do not create purpose in our lives. Purpose is something that flows from deep within our inner core.

By midlife we have attached much meaning to our life, but we may not have yet found our purpose. True self-esteem is related to our sense of purpose. There are no magic formulas for finding purpose. We find it by following our inner voice.

The problem with listening to the inner voice is that we don't know how to do this. If we have always done what everyone else wanted us to do, we may have buried our inner voice so deep inside that we do not know how to listen to it. We do not know how to find our purpose.

The great mythologist Joseph Campbell gave us some clues on how to do this. He suggested that the way to listen to our inner voice is *to make decisions without fear or desire*. If we do this, we have found a pathway to our inner voice. To have the courage to make our decisions on anything other than *fear* or *desire* is to act with the utmost integrity and to live with the highest self-esteem possible.

Following the inner voice is much more difficult than following the crowd. That is why very few people do it. In midlife, no one else can reflect our purpose—it must come from our inner soul. Others may help us find it and be encouraging, but ultimately the inner voice comes from deep inside. Looking in the mirror to find it is even more difficult than finding and owning the dark side within us.

A NEW LOOK AT THE MIRROR OF SELF-ESTEEM

When people are young, they become the image that others have helped make them out to be. During midlife comes a reshaping of the image of what we *really* are. Midlife is a time when we can become who we really are, and not just the image we have accepted ourselves to be.

Why is it in the middle years that we become concerned about the purpose and meaning of life? Can't we do this sooner? The first half of life is spent building a strong ego. It involves getting an education, forming a family, and developing a career. All of these consume our time. During the second half of life, the time comes for something else. The questions of purpose and the meaning of life itself are what the first half of life builds up to. By the middle years we can begin to focus on our purpose and incorporate this which always enhances our feelings about ourselves.

SOME ADDITIONAL PRACTICAL CONCRETE SUGGESTIONS

1. Accept the tension of opposites as part of life. Honor both sides of this tension and seek to maintain a balanced life. One example given in this chapter was the puer/puella and the senex tension. Consciously try to live life not as a puer/puella nor a senex. Work toward achieving a life that accepts and experiences both.

2. Welcome the physical changes the aging process brings. If physical attractiveness is what your self-esteem has been based on, develop other areas of your personality, such as inner beauty, which is just as important as physical attractiveness.

3. Determine if your job in some way supports your purpose in life. This does not mean that your job *IS* your purpose, but does it contribute to it? For example, if volunteer work is your calling in life, does the job you have provide enough pleasure and money to support your purpose? If not, determine what steps you need to take to make a career which in some way contributes to your purpose in life.

4. Examine your intimate relationships and determine if they are authentic. Were choices made realistically, or were they made to please other people? Work toward making your relationships real or seek to find those that will be mutually satisfying.

5. Remember to use your dark side to improve your self-esteem. Find out what you do not like about yourself by looking at what you do not like in others. Then find ways to use this information in a constructive way to broaden your self-esteem.

6. Stop trying to buy self-esteem. Self-esteem cannot be bought—it can only be reflected. Everyone is responsible for his or her own self-esteem. When you like what you see, others will reflect this.

7. Find your true purpose in life by making decisions which are *NOT* based on fear or desire. Your purpose cannot be fulfilled by anyone but you and only you can discover what that purpose is. An important way to find your purpose is to reflect over your own decisions—always looking for windows where fear and desire have crept in.

OTHER RESOURCES TO HELP YOU FOLLOW UP WHAT YOU LEARNED IN THIS CHAPTER

Bly, Robert. *A Little Book on the Human Shadow.* San Francisco: Harper & Row, 1988.

To better understand your dark side and what it has to do with self-esteem, read this book. Robert Bly explains how the shadow is formed in early life and what we can do about it in midlife.

Johnson, Robert. *Owning Your Own Shadow.* San Francisco: Harper San Francisco, 1991.

Like Robert Bly's book, this resource can help you better understand your dark side. Practical suggestions are provided about what to do with the shadow element of our personality.

Kiley, Dan. *The Peter Pan Syndrome: Men Who Have Never Grown Up.* New York: Avon Books, 1983.

This book sheds light on the puer or eternal child syndrome. It effectively describes men who do not want to grow up and explains why and what can be done about it.

Lewis, C. S. *Till We Have Faces.* San Diego: Harcourt Brace Jovanovich, 1957.

C. S. Lewis' novel is about a woman's journey into self-esteem. It shows how a woman finds her purpose and inner beauty after a long life of caring for others.

Pearson, Carol. *The Hero Within: Six Archetypes We Live By.* San Francisco: Harper & Row, 1986.

The hero's journey can take many patterns and forms. Carol Pearson explains how the hero may experience the feeling of being an orphan, a caretaker, a warrior, an innocent, a leader, and a magician. This book is especially recommended for women as they search for self-esteem.

CHAPTER NINE

DEVELOPING SELF-ESTEEM IN LATER ADULTHOOD

(SIXTY PLUS)

Self-esteem is challenged on many fronts late in life. Many factors contribute to self-worth or lack of it when we reach old age. Such things as retirement, changing environments, loss of friends and loved ones, and in some cases declining health can all impact on our self-worth. Senior adults who continue to develop self-esteem have some of the following personality traits.

1. *They tend to define themselves beyond work and develop interests and hobbies that sustain them.* Up until retirement many people (particularly men) have defined their self-worth in terms of how well they did their jobs or how successful they have been in the work force. Self-esteem after retirement requires a new orientation to self, separate from work. Adults who tend to have the highest self-esteem in later life are those who have been able to define themselves in ways other than their jobs. This does not mean they are no longer contributing or productive members of society. The direction of this contribution, though, has changed. The following two examples show the contrast.

Robert was a successful factory worker for over forty years.

When he retired he moved to another community. He and some of his other retired friends decided to open a specialty book shop. They each arranged it so they could work when they wanted to but were also fortunate enough to have the resources to hire workers for the book shop. Now Robert can work when he wants to but also has time for travel or relaxation and other interests. Robert enjoyed his job at the factory but no longer depends on this to give him feelings of self-worth. He opened the book shop as a hobby, but he does not base his self-esteem on the business either. His many other interests occupy his time and he does what he enjoys.

Jake is a retired businessman. For over thirty years he owned his own small business. When he retired he sold it. He still defines himself in terms of his business and insists on visiting his former place of work on a daily basis. He gives parties for the people who worked for him but is increasingly upset when many do not attend. What is worse, he is seldom included by his former workers in their social plans. He resents this and wonders what is wrong. Jake still defines himself in terms of work and is included less and less in the circle of his former world. This has had a negative effect on his self-regard.

2. *They have a self-concept that transcends constant worry about aches and pains and bodily deterioration.* Late in life, health may begin to decline. People with high self-esteem attend to their health care but are not continually preoccupied with the aging process. They are able to transcend this issue and have a positive attitude toward themselves even when they may not feel good.

Margaret is a retired secretary who has severe arthritis. Rather than give up, she volunteers regularly at the local soup kitchen. She cannot serve the food or wash the dishes because of her arthritis. This, however, has not stopped her from volunteering. She talks with the homeless and occasionally will organize programs for them. She encourages them to not give up and serves as a good role model for this. After all, Margaret has not given up.

3. *They are able to accept the inevitability of death so that they*

can live each day with grace to the fullest. Old age is a time to reflect on life and accept that death is a normal developmental part of life—just as much a part of it as the birth process. This allows them to take time to plan ahead by writing a will, getting a burial policy, planning a funeral and completing other tasks associated with death, if they have not done so earlier. While many senior adults live in memories of the past and some are preoccupied with death in the future, those with the highest self-esteem maintain some balance between these two extremes.

Joe is an example of living life to the fullest in the face of death. He is an eighty-year-old retired salesman who has lost three members of his family recently. His wife, a sister, and a brother have all died within the last year. Many people in Joe's situation would feel like giving up and dying too, but not Joe. While he developed a will and prepared for his burial over twenty years ago, Joe is still living. He is now planning a pleasure fishing trip with the few buddies that are still living, and he is even contemplating dating again.

4. *They value the importance of relationships with others.* Older people tend to define success in old age in terms of their relationships with others—the ability to get along. They are much less concerned about physical attributes such as attractiveness or self-knowledge than they are with relationships. The key word here is "relationships" and not "dependence." Continuing to enjoy family and friends is vital to self-esteem later in life.

Rita is a retired news reporter who has no living family members. Yet Rita is involved in building relationships. She moved into a multi-age apartment complex because she loves people—people of all ages. She especially likes children and baby sits regularly when she wants to. There are many opportunities for Rita to build relationships in her complex. There are many single working parents who trust and admire Rita, and she is included in many of their social circles. She did not give up when her family died. She continues to make friends, have a purposeful life, and maintain her self-esteem with the relationship that she created with the people around her.

5. *They are able to accept things as they are.* Older people with high self-esteem report that they are unhappy about virtually nothing. They accept the many changes that have occurred or are occurring as part of life and welcome fate as a friend.

Gay Nell has retired as a hostess at a restaurant. She has lived in her community for over sixty-five years. Her only daughter lives three-thousand miles away. This daughter has encouraged Gay Nell to come and live with her. Gay Nell's roots are in her community. She has her own life, and her daughter has her own life to live. Gay Nell has a strong support system through the many friends she met at the restaurant and community over the years. She has decided not to move far away where her daughter lives, and Gay Nell accepts the fact that her daughter will not move back to her community.

6. *They have a spiritual life of some kind.* This does not imply a religious orientation or church attendance, but adults who value themselves also value a higher source in guiding their later years. They honor this source and some form of prayer and communication is part of their spiritual development. Their self-esteem development is enhanced by their spiritual journey.

Eighty-year-old Jack has never been much of a religious man. However, in his later years he takes time every day to write in a journal and reflect over the little pleasures of life. He is thankful to God for his life, although he was never very successful—changing careers often during his earlier years. He has joined a literary society and finds it to be a spiritual experience as he and the group search for metaphors through books he enjoys. Jack is sustained by a spiritual attitude, even though he does not consider himself as a religious man.

7. *They accept the necessary changes in living arrangements.* Contrary to popular belief, most older adults live in the community (as opposed to a nursing home) and maintain their residence well into later adulthood. However, when a more streamlined environ-

ment is necessary or a change in living situations, those who like themselves are better able to cope and adjust to these changes. Just as they have learned to develop hobbies and interests beyond their previous jobs (and have stopped defining themselves in terms of their careers) they also do not define themselves in terms of where they live or how large their house is.

Michael is an eighty-year-old widower. For over forty years he and his wife owned a large two-story house with an acre of land. On his own, Michael decided that this large house was no longer a necessity for his ego. He sold the house, making enough money to buy a small condominium with enough left over to travel often and not worry about taking care of a large home and an acre of land. He has made friends with a neighboring widow at his new residence. He sometimes misses "the old home place" as he calls it. However, he lives life in the present as much as possible and enjoys life.

8. *They are able to handle life's problems without guilt, blame, or withdrawal.* Changes often come quickly. Those who can, learn to accept these without being bitter. The mirror of self-esteem in later life is the image or attitude a person has developed toward the world. Those who are most hostile or depressed about the outer world are reflecting their true feelings about their inner selves.

Martha is a seventy-eight year old whose only son is in prison for armed robbery. She still loves him and visits him weekly. She went through a long period of guilt and withdrawal from her friends. She wonders what she did. Martha, though, has always had relatively high self-esteem, and over time she began to accept that she did the best job she could in raising her son and has rejoined her friends and society. She is also a volunteer helper in a support group for family members of prisoners.

9. *They are able to accept losses such as the death of a spouse or friends.* This period can be a time of severe loss or separation— especially with regard to friends and loved ones. Those who are able to cope best have developed and maintained their own identi-

ties and have not seen themselves as extensions of their spouse, family, or friends. The losses are painful and felt deeply and should be experienced as such. However, each person in later life is still an individual and those who have maintained this individuality and uniqueness are able to see themselves apart from their losses.

Maryann is a sixty-five-year-old retired social worker. Just two years ago her husband died suddenly of a heart attack. While she had worked most of her life, her husband had always taken care of business affairs. In fact, Maryann had never written a check until her husband died. She felt like giving up, but with the help of a friend learned how to manage her own business affairs. She still misses her husband but knows she is able to take care of herself. Maryann admits it was her self-esteem which played a big part in her not giving up and becoming helpless.

10. *Finally, those with highest self-regard see themselves as contributing to society in some way.* This contribution may have been in the past, but they can look back with pride upon their accomplishments and successes and accept the place to which it has brought them.

One example of a contributing member of society is George. George is a retired farmer who never became rich from his land. However, he was very active in his community and church. He helped start a half-way house for the mentally retarded several years before retirement and takes pride in this and other civic and volunteer accomplishments in his younger days. He feels he made his contribution, and indeed he has.

SOME MORE PRACTICAL CONCRETE SUGGESTIONS FOR DEVELOPING AND MAINTAINING SELF-ESTEEM IN LATE ADULTHOOD

There are two ways to approach suggestions for building self-esteem later in life. One way is to make suggestions for older people themselves. The other way is to recommend ways we can help the elderly build self-esteem. Both of these ways are accounted for here.

What the Elderly Can Do for Themselves

The following ideas are given for ways you can build and keep your self-esteem late in life:

1. ***Develop interests and hobbies which will sustain you during your retirement.*** Learn to define yourself in ways other than your previous career.

2. ***Tend to your health care needs*** through exercise, nutrition, and maintenance but do not be consumed with the aging process. Learn to accept the fact that we are more than our bodies.

3. ***Work toward accepting that death is a normal part of the life cycle.*** How can you do this? How a person prepares for death and how to deal with it is an individual issue. Some develop their spirituality, others sort out their affairs, while others work on reflecting over their life. Those with higher self-worth late in life are able to come to terms in some way with approaching death.

4. ***Enjoy the companionship of others.*** Intimacy is an important aspect of self-esteem in the elderly. Do your part to develop and maintain true communication and authentic relationships. Work toward harmony. Senior adults often report harmony in relationships as important to their self-esteems. Sometimes this is not possible. When it is not, value that you have done your part and accept the turn that relationships take.

5. ***Accept the twists and turns of fate.*** Those with the highest self-worth late in life are able to roll with the punches. Learn the difficult task of finding out what you do and do not have control over. Then do your part to change the things you can and gracefully accept what life brings in terms of things you cannot change.

6. *Develop a spiritual life.* During the second half of life it is necessary to attend to the issues of the soul to develop self-esteem fully. Do not depend on others for your own spiritual development. Others may be a source of help or inspiration, but your own spiritual development, just as your own sense of self-worth, is your personal responsibility throughout life.

7. *Accept necessary changes in living arrangements.* It is best to prepare ahead for these changes if and when they come. Those with high self-regard are able to make it through the various changing environments in which they find themselves.

8. *Develop an attitude about the world that does not result in or from blame, withdrawal, or guilt.* The attitude you have toward life is a direct reflection of your self-esteem in later life.

9. *Maintain your individuality.* Enjoy friends, spouses, and family but do not count on them to define who you are or provide you with a positive self-image. This comes from within—especially later in life. Define who you are independent of others.

10. *Continue to contribute to society as long as you can.* When this is no longer possible, take pride in the contributions you have already made or at least attempted to make. Look back with pride at your commitments and choices and honor yourself for making a difference.

How You Can Help the Elderly Enhance Their Self-esteem

The following are suggestions for ways other people can help the elderly develop self-esteem:

1. *Treat senior adults like adults.* Treat them with respect even when they are incapable of taking care of themselves. No matter what their capacity for understanding they still have esteem needs.

2. *Work WITH the elderly as much as possible and not FOR them.* The aged have a need for autonomy. Whenever possible, allow them to govern their own lives and make their own decisions.

3. *Let the elderly do things in their own way.* Respect the older adult's individuality. While allowing them to make decisions and do for themselves, remember that they have their own way of doing things.

4. *Respect the older adult's need for privacy.* When they become in need of additional care, remember that they still have esteem needs related to their own possessions. Respect their property.

5. *Listen to the elderly, even when it is difficult.* Very late in life when their short-term memory begins to fail, try to understand their need for expression. Set aside time to listen to what they have to say.

6. *Support the elderly in periods of crisis.* There are many losses in later life. Seek ways to be helpful without robbing their autonomy.

7. *Help the elderly find recreational outlets.* Often community or church organizations provide this.

8. *Teach the elderly to turn their troubles into blessings.* For example, if they cannot sleep, suggest they read or find something else to do.

9. *Encourage them to keep a journal or write their memoirs.* This can help build self-esteem by keeping them in touch with their inner life.

OTHER RESOURCES TO HELP YOU FOLLOW UP WHAT YOU LEARNED IN THIS CHAPTER

Biracree, T., and Biracree, N. *Over Fifty: The Resource Book for the Better Half of Your Life.* New York: Harper, 1991.

This book describes how to get the most out of your relationships, work, and family during the second half of life. Practical suggestions are made throughout the book.

Neugarten, Bernice. *Middle Ages and Aging.* Chicago: University of Chicago Press, 1968.

This volume by one of the world's foremost experts on adulthood and aging describes the developmental changes of aging in the areas of intellectual, emotional, and physical development.

Rose, X. *Widow's Journey: A Return to the Loving Self.* New York: Holt, 1990.

By the time people are in their eighties there are ten women for every man. This book describes one person's struggle with self-esteem after widowhood. Since there are so many widows in the later quarter of life, this is a recommended resource on how to take care of yourself as a widow.

CHAPTER TEN

SELF-ESTEEM AND THE DISABLED*

Our study of self-esteem would be incomplete without considering special situations. One of these is the disabled and their families. In this chapter we will consider how a disabled child influences the self-esteem of family members and how a disabled person can build self-esteem themselves.

ESTEEM NEEDS OF FAMILIES WHO HAVE DISABLED CHILDREN

Parenting a disabled child can test a person's self-worth in many ways. The reaction to having a special child can throw us into any number of emotions including shock, denial, hope, grief, anger, or guilt. One reason for the flood of emotional reactions is the idea of the perfect child. When we are expecting a baby we most often think of having the perfect child. Feelings about ourselves are tested when an exceptional child is born. We learn much about our-

---

*Many people prefer the term "differently abled" to "disabled." I am using the term "disabled" because it is most often used in local, state, and federal programs for the "differently abled."

125

selves and life from the experience the disabled child can teach us.

A disabled child may have special needs such as extra efforts at caregiving and medical needs far beyond the typical child. The special child may impact our marriage, our family activities, our social involvement, and our self-esteem. This, however, does not have to be negative. If we have sufficient self-esteem and coping abilities we can make it.

Families who seem to cope best are those whose members have a high regard for themselves and the disabled child. Families who cope best also communicate openly and freely, expressing their own feelings. They share responsibilities and integrate the child into family life. Parents who feel good about their roles do not attend to this child at the expense of the other children nor do they neglect the special child. They feel comfortable with their roles and try to maintain a family balance. Parents with a strong liking for themselves are not embarrassed by the situation and accept and adapt as best they can.

Research shows quite convincingly that the major difference between parents with high self-esteem and parents with low self-worth who have disabled children involves the issues of *guilt, overprotection,* and *advocacy.* Parents with low self-esteem are much more likely to feel guilty and blame themselves for their child's condition. They may be overprotective and fail to teach the child social skills. They may even neglect needed services such as physical therapy if the child protests that it is too painful. Parental low self-esteem, guilt, and overprotection are destructive forces impeding the growth, development, and learning of the family members.

Parents with high self-esteem believe in themselves and their disabled child. They act as advocates for their children's rights even when professionals disagree. JoAnn is the mother of a twenty-eight-year-old Down Syndrome son named Joe. She feels good about herself. She believes in herself, and she believes in Joe.

Consequently, she has always been his advocate. When he became sixteen she lobbied for him to receive a driver's license. He passed both the written and driving test and was awarded a license. She helped him find a job, and he now lives independently as a contributing member of society. JoAnn's self-esteem was a contributing factor in Joe's independence today.

JoAnn was also an advocate for her son during his school years. Although we now have laws which require a free appropriate education for all disabled children, the education of special children is still based on a deficit rather than a strength model. This means we focus on what the child can *NOT* do and focus on this. What we should be doing is finding their strengths and capitalizing on them. Parental advocacy for the rights of the exceptional in education, jobs, and community living requires an enormous amount of self-esteem. This self-esteem pays off for the parents, the child and society in general.

SELF-ESTEEM NEEDS OF THE DISABLED

Disabled children and adults need a healthy self-worth to cope with society as well. The general population has a long way to go in understanding and accepting the disabled. Disabled individuals who have the highest self-esteem are advocates for themselves. *One of the strongest esteem needs of the disabled is to learn how to be advocates for themselves.*

Although laws prohibit it, the disabled are often subjected to misunderstandings and discrimination. Holly, a woman with cerebral palsy went to renew her driver's license. She was denied the renewal on the basis of how she looked. The denying officer admitted it! He failed to renew her license because of how she looked. If Holly had low self-esteem she would have accepted this decision, but instead she went to a lawyer and had her license reinstated. Her positive self-regard allowed her to be her own advocate.

FIVE SELF-ESTEEM RULES FOR THE DISABLED
AND/OR THEIR FAMILIES

The suggestions already made throughout this book all apply to the disabled and their families. However, seven additional suggestions are made specifically for helping build self-esteem. These include:

1. *Communicate openly.* Express your feelings and needs and listen to other family members as they communicate their needs.

One example of open communication is the Martin family. Curtis and Beth Martin have four children. Their oldest son Bill is fifteen and has severe cerebral palsy. They also have an eleven-year-old son and twin daughters who are eight. The Martins have always talked openly about their situation and encouraged Bill's siblings to do the same. Up until recently, the younger son shared a room with Bill. Now that he is in middle school he wants more privacy and was free to communicate this with the family. Unfortunately, the house the Martins live in has only three bedrooms, but since communication was so open they frequently discussed possible solutions. The family saved their money to turn the garage into a fourth bedroom and are in the process of implementing this plan.

2. *Participate in a balanced life as much as possible.* The birth of a disabled child can throw family participation out of balance. Self-esteem, though, grows out of a balanced life.

A good example of a family who strives to maintain a balanced life is the Carter family. Jessica and Charles Carter have an autistic child. Their five-year-old daughter Cindy could take all of their time if they would let her.

By the time Cindy was three, Jessica realized that she was no longer a participating member of the community. In fact, she spent all of her time caring for Cindy. Cindy's behavior was too unpredictable to leave her with a baby sitter or enroll her in a day care. Jessica, though, wanted to have some time for herself. What could she do? Jessica contacted a friend who taught special education in the local school system. Her friend informed her that there are now programs required by federal law for all three to five year olds who have severe disabilities. Jessica contacted the local school board and enrolled Cindy in such a program. Now Jessica has time for herself every day (during school hours) to take a part-time job or rejoin some of the organizations she quit after Cindy's birth. She now talks about being a better mother for Cindy since she has some time for her own needs.

3. *Make a plan to deal with guilt and blame.* Guilt and blame are destructive emotions. These are harmful not only to your own self-esteem but to the well being of others.

Paula is an example of a parent who suffers from guilt and blame. She is a very religious woman who blames herself for her eight-year-old son choking on a hot dog. Because her son, Phil, almost died before the hot dog was dislodged from his throat, he now has severe brain damage.

At first Paula blamed herself for Phil's condition. She had decided that she must be punished for Phil's condition and proceeded to do everything for him—until she had a nervous breakdown. Paula is now receiving professional help from a counselor to deal with her guilt and pain. She is learning that guilt and blame are of no help to her or her son. She has stopped doing everything for him and is working on helping him move toward more independence. Paula's counselor is helping her build self-esteem so that she can be a better mother to Phil.

4. *Be an advocate for yourself and your child.* Take a stand when you know what is best for you and your family. JoAnn who was mentioned earlier in this chapter is a good example of how to be an advocate for your child. Margaret is an example of how to be an advocate for yourself.

Margaret is a woman in her mid-forties who is taking her own journey in life against all odds. She is the mother of three children ranging in age from nine to sixteen. Her middle child, Joan, is deaf.

Margaret works for the rights of her deaf daughter, but she also works hard for her own right to develop a career.

Margaret is pursuing her PhD. at a university ninety miles from her home. She stays on campus three days a week and tends to her family responsibilities the rest of the week. Her husband is a traditionalist who believes the woman's place is in the home taking care of kids—especially if one of them has special needs. Her children would prefer her to be home all week too. Margaret is her own person and does what she needs to do for herself as well as her family. Although she occasionally feels guilty, she is doing what she needs to do.

Margaret has not always followed her heart. When she was a teenager she wanted to be a physician but thought, "I can't do that. Women are not doctors." While Margaret did not follow her original calling, she is following her heart now—even with a disabled child. Her husband and family are learning to be more responsible while she is away, and Margaret's advocacy for herself is slowly paying off.

5. *Look for your strengths and the strengths of your child.* Remember that the education of the disabled is often based on their weaknesses instead of their strengths. Communicate with teachers and friends the positive aspects and strengths of your child.

Bob is a single father who was told his learning disabled son Tom would never read. Bob did not believe this and began reading to his child every night before bed. He also points out logos and environmental print to Tom when they are in the car or in the grocery store. Tom has started recognizing labels and road signs. Bob is working on Tom's strengths which include a natural curiosity about his surroundings. Bob is using this to help Tom begin to read. Tom's teacher should be doing the same.

We are all alike and different in some ways. A disability is just one way that we may be different. Self-esteem development may take more work when a disability exists in the family, but higher self-esteem can be achieved by all who truly seek it.

OTHER RESOURCES TO HELP YOU FOLLOW UP WHAT YOU LEARNED IN THIS CHAPTER

Krents, Harold. *To Race the Wind: The Vibrant Testament of a Blind Boy Who Tackled Life Head-On.* New York: Bantam, 1972.

This is the story of how self-esteem can make the difference in someone with a disability. It is the story of a blind man who became a cum laude graduate of Harvard, as well as a person with numerous hobbies including songwriting and playing football.

Long, Kate. *Johnny's Such a Bright Boy, What a Shame He's Retarded.* Boston: Houghton Mifflin, 1977.

Some children are wrongly identified as retarded. This book describes how children can be sent to special education classes when they do not need it and what parents and teachers can do about this dilemma.

Orlansky, Michael, and Heward, William. *Voices: Interviews with Handicapped People.* Columbus, OH: Merrill, 1981.

There are numerous types of exceptionality. These include physical, emotional, intellectual, and sensory disabilities. Orlansky and Heward interviewed people from each of these types of disability. Their stories of self-esteem can be used to inspire others who are also differently abled.

CHAPTER ELEVEN

SELF-ESTEEM AND THE GROUP

Self-esteem is not only individual, but we share in the self-esteem of both the culture and our country. We all share with others the feelings of pride we have in our nation and heritage. The group self-esteem influences and reflects our own self-regard. There are many positive feelings we share with others and many which are not so positive.

In the United States we can feel good about the many *freedoms* we enjoy. The bill of rights preserves our right to enjoy self-worth with others. This includes freedom of religion, freedom to assemble, voting privileges, and so on. The individual freedoms guaranteed us are also shared and valued by others. It is all part of our "group" self-esteem.

We also hold many *privileges* which sustain our group self-esteem. The opportunity for an education and highways to take us where we want to go enhance our abilities to explore both the inner and outer worlds we live in. Even when we are wrong, we have a right to a fair trial and, if possible, the choice of who will represent us. We not only share freedoms, we share privileges.

We can also share in the giving and receiving of charitable and nonprofit organizations. Everything from the Jerry Lewis Telethon for Muscular Dystrophy to the aid provided by the Salvation Army is part of the positive side of the group. In every town and city there are community and religious groups we can be a part of to share what we have with others.

We also share in the negative aspects of the group. This is the group shadow or dark side. If we are to build the group self-esteem we must face these negative aspects as well as the positive ones. It is not unpatriotic, cynical, or defeating to see the dark side, but it is very difficult to acknowledge our group shadow. Only by doing so, can we truly have shared self-esteem.

Just as we project our individual shadows on to others (by attributing to them the things we do not like about ourselves), we also project our collective shadows as well. Up until recently, we projected our shadow on to the Soviet Union, and they attributed their dark side to us. With these projections withdrawn we must now attend to the painful task of owning our own problems and acknowledging them.

We remember Nazi Germany well and the terrible crimes of the holocaust. We must acknowledge our own holocaust in which we destroyed many Native American nations. We rationalize and say it was different or the number of people are not the same. We must own our own crimes in order to rebuild our nation's self-esteem. We must remember or the destruction will spiral around again.

We currently project the AIDS epidemic on the "other" people. The disease belongs to homosexuals or I.V. drug users or prostitutes or Haitians. We must admit it is everyone's problem or it will destroy us.

We have a long road ahead of us in facing our difficult issues of the homeless, child care, education, health care, the rights of women, the disabled, the elderly, and homosexuals. These are all controversial issues, and I do not hold the answer. I only know that if we do not face them we cannot have a healthy group self-esteem. These are all difficult issues because they are part of our group shadow.

Just what does all of this have to do with our own individual self-esteem? The group mirrors our individuality, and we in turn mirror the group. We do not live in a vacuum. The group decisions impact on all of us. We, in a smaller sense influence the nation. Just as we can never truly love ourselves unless we recognize our own shadows and stop projecting them, the United States can never feel good (collectively) unless each of us recognizes his or her own problems and attempts to deal with them.

We recognize our economic problems. We are taught to follow this very closely. There is, of course, nothing wrong with this. We do it well, but it has drawn us into an imbalanced attention on money. Economics cannot buy self-esteem. This makes us uneasy because we somehow recognize this. We laugh about this because we make jokes about what makes us uncomfortable. I have an uncle who said, "I know money won't buy happiness, but it can purchase a satin pillow for me to cry on." If our nation neglects spiritual values then this mirrors the condition we find in our own individual lives. If the country denies its plurality then we lose our individuality.

SUGGESTIONS FOR BUILDING CULTURAL AND NATIONAL SELF-ESTEEM

1. *Share in the positive aspects of the culture.* There is much of which to be proud.
2. *Take advantage of opportunities to grow which the nation provides.* Follow your heart and contribute to the decision-making process of the community in which you live.
3. *Contribute to the well-being of others through volunteer or charitable work.* Give something back by giving of time to a support group, nursing home, day care, or other volunteer capacity.
4. *Acknowledge our national and cultural tragedies.* Feel the sorrow of our own holocaust so that history will not repeat itself, and cause us to inflict pain upon others.

5. *Participate in the group process by voting and expressing your conscience.* Make a difference in national self-esteem by participating and contributing your voice to the larger group.

SELF-ESTEEM AND CULTURAL DIVERSITY

We not only live in a culture which influences our self-esteem, we all live in a subculture which must be honored as well. Most of us have heard that the United States is the great melting pot. This provides a depressing image for our self-esteem. We see ourselves thrown together—all coming out just alike. A better way to look at America is to see it as a salad bowl.*

The image of a salad bowl provides a picture of each individual part or culture contributing something rich and needed for the overall culture at large. Each individual culture maintains its own identity just like the tomatoes, lettuce, and celery are identifiable in a salad—yet they all contribute to the flavor and richness.

If we truly accept ourselves we can value other people from various cultures and customs and not be threatened by them. **A true sign of low self-esteem is the inability to accept other people and other cultures.** If we are secure and like ourselves, we can be open to learning about other people's values without feeling our own ways will suffer.

In the past we tried to make everyone conform to the broader culture. If we look closely at why this happened we will see it was because of our own insecurities. We were saying, the more you are like us the better you will feel. What we were feeling is, the more you are like us the better *WE* will feel.

A good example of this was our inability to accept the Native Americans as a valued culture. When Mabel, an English teacher, went to teach in Western North Carolina in the 1930s she was told

* I am thankful to my colleague Dr. Stephen Graves for providing me with this metaphor.

to burn all of the Cherokee literature and teach only standard English. She saved Native American resources she found and was able to preserve them and return them later to the Cherokee nation.

I have given speeches at Puerto Rican universities in the past. Unfortunately, I am not fluent enough in Spanish to give lectures in that language. During one of my conferences in San Juan a gentleman spoke with me and apologized for not being able to understand English very well. I expressed that I was the one who should apologize. I had come to his island and did not know the language.

I am particularly concerned about the lack of African American characters in children's literature. I was recently listening to a black female psychologist who was expounding on this problem. She had been working with a young girl who was upset because she did not feel she could be a princess in the school play. When asked, "Why not?" she responded, "There are no black princesses."

I have seen similar behaviors in my own college classes. I teach a course on children's literature and require my students to write and illustrate their own children's book. In one of my recent classes I had nine African American women in the class. None of them included black children in their original story illustrations!

SOME PRACTICAL SUGGESTIONS FOR BUILDING YOUR SUBCULTURAL SELF-ESTEEM

1. *Value your own culture and take pride in your cultural heritage.*
2. *Accept other cultures and learn from them.* Remember, to accept yourself, accept others.

SELF-ESTEEM AND WOMEN

The changing roles of women poses questions and issues for them about their self-esteem. While the majority of women are now participating in the work force, expectations of their roles may be lagging behind. For example, husbands often leave child care and household chores to their wives even when their wives work full-time. The divided loyalties a woman endures places stress on her self-worth.

Suzanne is a woman in her mid-fifties who is taking her own journey in life. She is the mother of two teenagers who are fourteen and sixteen. Suzanne is pursuing her law degree at a university 110 miles from her home. Her husband, like Margaret's husband, is a traditionalist who believes the woman's place is in the home.

Suzanne has always wanted to be a lawyer and is now pursuing this dream. She is learning to give up her perfectionist tendencies and avoid the super woman syndrome. She is seeking to meet her own needs as well as attend to her family's.

SUGGESTIONS FOR WOMEN IN BUILDING THEIR OWN SELF-ESTEEM

1. *Accept that you have a life of your own.* Live it authentically and do not base your decisions on fear or desire.
2. *Do not define yourself in terms of others.* You may be a wife, a mother and have a career, but these are only parts of you. Define yourself in terms of who you are to yourself. You can start by listing your good qualities, without mentioning other people.
3. *Ask for help from others when you need it.* Avoid the super woman syndrome. You have a right to have your needs met just as anyone else.

OTHER RESOURCES TO HELP YOU FOLLOW UP WHAT YOU LEARNED IN THIS CHAPTER

Carter, Forrest. *The Education of Little Tree.* Albuquerque: University of New Mexico Press, 1976.

This book describes the journey of a native American boy in the 1930s and how his culture and self-esteem helped him through difficult times.

Lee, Harper. *To Kill a Mockingbird.* New York: Warner, 1960.

This classic book describes a how a young girl learns to accept individual and cultural diversity. She learns from her father's example that all human beings are worthy of respect.

Stone, Merlin. *When God Was a Woman.* San Diego: Harcourt Brace Jovanovich, 1976.

In many ancient civilizations, God was considered to be feminine. Ms. Stone traces the roots of religion back to a matriarchy.

Chapter Twelve

CONCLUSIONS— DECISIONS FOR SELF-ESTEEM

As we have seen throughout this book, self-esteem is a lifelong process. It is a spiral and a mirror; general and specific; individual and collective. Our behaviors, attitudes, evaluations, and motivations influence and are influenced by our self-worth. Whether we choose to develop it or not, self-esteem can be improved. We can move from an outer influence to an inner one until we become fully responsible for our own self-worth.

SEVEN DECISIONS TO MAKE

This entire book has been about making decisions to build self-esteem. Although there are many suggestions throughout the book, seven overall or general recommendations can be made for improving your self-esteem over time.

1. *Make a commitment to work on your self-esteem.* Some things which might help include keeping a journal or seeking help through therapy or counseling. Self-esteem involves reflection. Set aside time to consider your behaviors, attitudes, how you evaluate your self, and what motivates you. Low self-esteem is easier to

confirm and maintain than the commitment to work on high self-esteem. Make the needed effort to change.

2. *Follow your inner voice.* Take your journey. This journey is a psychological one. Many people have lost the ability to hear their inner voice because they have done what others have wanted them to do for so long. You know you are following your inner voice when you make decisions which are important to you.

You make these decisions not based on fear or desire. The journey directed by your inner voice may take you around the world, but the journey is internal. You need not even leave your house to begin it.

3. *Listen to other people's evaluations of you to see if they are reflecting your own feelings of self-worth.* This may seem like a contradiction of the second recommendation. Some people have listened to others for so long they cannot hear their own inner voice. Once we start to listen to the inner voice, we can check it against others' reflections. As adults, others most often reflect our own true feelings. Others often see us as we see ourselves.

4. *Don't accept the value judgments of others.* These statements come in various forms such as, "You're ugly, stupid, or uninteresting." When people accept the value judgments from others they live them out. Fortunately, I did not listen to my eighth grade math teacher. When I was in eighth grade my family moved to another community. I was failing eighth grade math, and my mother went to talk with my teacher about it. He said, "I wouldn't worry about it. Your son is probably retarded." Thirteen years later I was teaching a graduate course. The first day I looked out across my students, and there was my eighth grade math teacher—taking my class.

5. *Accept the dark side of your personality.* Everybody has one. Since life maintains a balance between the good and bad, the greater our potential for greatness, the more our potential for destruction as well. This does not mean to live out the dark side. Hitler is an example of someone who did. It means to recognize it so you WON'T live it out. When we are unconscious of our own dark sides, they are

more destructive than when we see them. It never ceases to amaze me how people are shocked when the tabloids point out the dark side of some famous person. Of course they all have dark sides, and they are in direct proportion to their positive attributes.

6. ***Do not project or accept blame and guilt.*** These are destructive emotions to ourselves and others. If they were productive in any way it would be different. We can feel anger, regret, remorse, and many other emotions and transfer guilt and blame to one of these. When something goes wrong we have a tendency to find or even invent blame. Most often we blame our self-esteem on our parents. All parents make mistakes, but as adults we are all responsible for our own self-worth. Guilt is also just as destructive. When we feel guilty for being rude or fat or selfish it does nothing to help the situations.

7. ***Accept responsibility for your own self-esteem.*** People who are overly concerned with what others think of them have poor self-esteem and a feeling of helplessness. They give others far too much credit. When we do not take responsibility for ourselves the thoughts of others overwhelm us.

Self-esteem is a lifelong process of becoming. We often want to know when we will get there, but the process of living life to its fullest is the process of building self-esteem. I close this book with the idea of both being and becoming. My own search for self-esteem is best expressed in the following thoughts recorded in my journal in March, 1991.

THE MAP MAKER

There was once a self-esteem map maker whose job was to design the most accurate of all road signs. The map maker was given many tools for his task. These included power, knowledge, and control. With these he began to prepare the most important of all maps—the one that people should follow.

He began with all power to draw the legend and scale so that no one would get lost. His knowledge of the many roads was vast, and he had learned how to control what he believed to be the future destinies of all who followed his creation. The use of power, knowledge, and control were the valued instruments of map preparation.

Soon the map was honored as the only possible roads in life, and the powers that be set in motion teaching people how to follow the map. All persons started at the same place and were sent forth to follow the guide. Soon those in authority became concerned. Some people were not progressing through their travels fast enough while others just blatantly ignored the guides.

Those who were not following the map were singled out as different and in need of correction. Soon a reward system was set up for those who followed this map of perfection. They were given the tools of the map maker for their efforts. These, of course, were power, knowledge, and control which were used to impose the map upon others.

Now the map maker had great talents but they were not put to good use. Power, knowledge, and control were exploited to perpetuate conformity. The ideas of purpose and wisdom and destiny were not part of the map maker's repertoire and so the map was worthless.

All of us know the map maker as he appears in various forms. Sometimes he shows up as a well-meaning parent who imposes the map on an innocent child. Sometimes he appears as a religious leader who attempts to impose a standard of values through those devices of power, knowledge, and control. Often he appears in schools as the curriculum giver who forces his way into the classroom with threats of testing, higher standards, and artificial goals. We've all seen him in many forms, and we are all too quick to follow this guide in a quest for self-esteem. We are too ready to give up the ideas of purpose, wisdom, and destiny.

It is all too easy to play the map maker's game for we are scared and fragile and fear being alone. We've forgotten the map that is inborn or the map maker's guide was given too early and our own maps never took form.

A new map maker is needed. True, we have our own maps within, but how do we find them? Why do we need a map maker? Imposed maps never help us arrive at our final destination. We need a map maker who is first of all in touch with the self-esteem within. Then we need to follow that map out of a center of purpose, wisdom, and a sense of destiny rather than the tradition of valued power, knowledge, and control. We need a map maker who respects the individual's ability to find the way, no matter how long the journey and no matter how painful.

We need not wait for the map maker to appear in politics, religion, the family, or education. Deep within us is that map maker, and we must all search first to find this healer deep within. Each of us must follow that map maker deep within our own psychological center. This takes courage, a bit of fear, and an initial sense of uncertainty. Those before us who have searched long and hard for life's purpose have found their efforts not in vain. The return to the exterior map maker was no longer possible.

INDEX

Activity level, 42
  (*see also* Temperament)
Adaptability, 43
  (*see also* Temperament)
Adjustment, 26, 85, 104-105
Adolescence, 20, 28, 30, 31, 37, 82-90
Advocacy, 126, 127, 129
African American(s), 136
Age group, 103
Aging parents, 103
AIDS, 133
Aldridge, Jerry, 63, 81
Amor and Psyche, 28
Antithetical relationship, 48
Approach-withdrawal, 43
  (see temperament)
Asocial stage, 40
  (*see also* Attachment)
Assault/schools, 54, 56, 58, 63
Attachment, 39-41
  (*see also* Bonding)
Attention span, 43
  (*see also* Temperament)

Attitude(s), 40, 45, 96, 116, 118, 119, 122
Autonomy, 44-45, 74, 123

Balanced life, 98-103
Barometric self-esteem, 83
Bates, Marilyn, 69
Bean, R., 72, 90
Beauty pageants, 28, 54, 61
Behavior(s), 20, 24, 80, 87, 90, 128
Biracree, Nancy, 123
Biracree, Thomas, 123
Blame, 92, 119, 122, 126, 129, 141
  (*see also* Guilt)
Blessings, 123
Bly, Robert, 107, 113
Bodily deterioration, 116
Bodily-kinesthetic, 69
  (*see also* Intelligences)
Bonding, 39
  (*see also* Attachment)
Boys, 24, 60, 77, 107
Braham, Barbara, 111
Brandon, Nathaniel, 97

Brazelton, Berry, 43
Bredekamp, Sue, 63
Briggs, Dorothy, 50
Buzzard group/reading, 59

Career(s), 30, 31, 86, 88-89, 93-94,
    97, 116-117
Caregivers, 40
Campbell, Joseph, 111
Carter, Forrest, 137
Charitable work, 134
    (*see also* Volunteer work)
Cherokee nation, 136
Chess, Stella, 42
Child care, 45, 51, 64, 133, 137
Children's temperament, 42-43, 49
Clark, Aminah, 90
Clemes, Harris, 72, 90
Clothing 34, 37, 54, 56, 62, 88
Commitment, 91, 96, 139
Companionship, 109, 121
Comparison(s), 27, 35
Compensatory experiences, 67, 68,
    72
Competition, 27, 28, 35
Complex, 26
Conflict, 34, 92
Conformity, 27, 29, 35, 142
Cultural heritage, 30, 33, 136
Cultural tragedies, 134
Curriculum, 142
Curry, Nancy, 50

Dark side, 107-113, 133-134
    (*see also* Shadow)
Death, 68, 116-117, 119-121
Decisions/for self-esteem, 123, 137,
    139-141
Defensiveness, 92
Demands, 76

Desire, 92, 105, 111, 113, 137, 140
Destiny, 28, 142-143
Development, 126
Developmental self-esteem, 21
Differently abled, 14, 125
Disabled, 125-131
Distractibility, 43
    (*see also* Temperament)
Doubt, 44, 46, 65
Down Syndrome, 126
Drawing, 26, 53, 63
Dusek, Jerome, 90

Early childhood, 52-63
Education, 112, 127, 129-133, 137,
    143
Elderly, 121-123
    (*see also* Later adulthood; Senior
    adults)
Elementary children, 70
    (*see also* Middle childhood;
    Preadolescence)
Elkind, David, 54-55, 59, 63
Emerson, Peggy, 40
Entrance examinations/for kinder-
    garten, 59
    (*see also* Testing)
Environment(s), 33, 37, 38, 40-41,
    80, 115, 122
Erikson, Erik, 44, 64
Ethnicity, 93
Evaluation(s), 20, 25, 87
Extraverts, 70
    (*see also* Typology)

Fairytales, 55
Family issues, 106
Family structure, 79
Fantasy life, 70
Fate, 118, 121

Fear, 19, 60, 85-86, 104, 109, 111, 113, 137, 140, 143
Feelers, 70
   (*see also* Typology)
Feeling(s), 20, 37
Flashcards, 55
   (*see also* Education)
Folktales, 55
Football, 24, 35, 55, 131
Fragmentation, 56, 58, 62
Freedom(s), 38, 46, 72, 132
   in middle childhood, 72
   in toddlers, 46
   in the United States, 132
   religious, 38
Friend(s)
   and the disabled, 129
   in adolescence, 83-14
   in early adulthood, 94
   in later adulthood, 115-120, 122
   in middle adulthood, 109
   in preadolescence, 75, 78

Gardner, Howard, 68-69, 73
Garfield, Charles, 93-94, 97
Girls, 55, 77, 107
   (*see also* Women)
Group
   play, 60
   self-esteem, 132-138
   shadow, 133-134
Guide, 142
Guilt, 119, 126, 141
   (*see also* Blame)
Haitians, 133
Hands-on learning, 57
   (*see also* Education)
Harter, Susan, 85
Health care, 116, 121, 133
Henderson, Lisa, 76

Heward, William, 131
Hobbies, 21, 30, 66, 72, 94, 119, 121, 131
Homecoming queen, 105
Homeless, 116, 133
Homogeneous grouping, 56, 59, 62
Homosexuals, 133
Hunt, Morton, 97

Indiscriminate attachment state, 40
   (*see also* Attachment)
Individual pursuits, 94
Individuality, 29
Infants, 39-51
   (*see also* Toddlers)
Informal peer groups, 74
Inner voice, 105, 111, 140
Intelligence(s), 26, 68, 69, 96
Intensity of reaction, 43
   (*see also* Temperament)
Interests, 71, 115, 119, 121
Interpersonal, 69
   (*see also* Intelligences)
Intimacy, 27, 91, 98, 106, 121
Intimate relationships, 21-22, 106
Intrapersonal, 69
   (*see also* Intelligences)
Introverts, 70
   (*see also* Typology)
Intuitives, 70
   (*see also* Typology)

Jacobson, Lenore, 73
Johnson, Carl, 50
Johnson, Robert, 113
Joy, 78
Jung, Carl, 45, 110

Keirsey, David, 69
Kiley, Dan, 114

Kindergarten, 26-27, 59, 62
(*see also* Early childhood)
Kohen-Raz, Reuven, 81
Kraus, Robert, 48
Krents, Harold, 131

Later adulthood, 115-124
Learned helplessness, 41
Learning, 58, 68-69, 72
    centers, 58
    experiences, 67
    station, 58
    styles, 68-69, 72
Lee, Harper, 137
Lewis, C. S., 114
Lifespan, 13, 15, 26, 91
Linguistic, 69
    (*see also* Intelligences)
Living arrangements, 118, 122
Long, Kate, 131
Love, 21, 25, 91

Manning, Gary, 56, 59, 63
Manning, Maryann, 56, 59, 63
Map, 15, 141-143
Marriage, 21-22, 92, 103
Mathematical-logical, 69
    (*see also* Intelligences)
May, Rollo, 97
Mead, George, H. 22
Meaning, 27, 110-111
    (*see also* Purpose)
Memoirs, 123
Menopause, 98, 103
Mentally ill parent, 68
Middle adulthood, 27, 30, 98-114
Middle childhood, 64-73
Midlife, 27, 38, 98, 103, 105-106
    crisis 98, 103, 106
    transition 27, 38, 105

trauma 103
Minuchin, Patricia, 81
Mirror, 22
Motivation(s), 20, 25, 139
Multiple attachments stage, 40
    (*see also* Attachment)
Musical, 69
    (*see also* Intelligences)
Muus, Rolf, 90
Myth, 28

Native Americans, 37-38, 133, 136
Nazi Germany, 133
Neugarten, Bernice, 124
Neumann, Eric, 63
Newborn, 40, 41, 48

Opposite sex relationships, 21
    (*see also* Sex)
Orlansky, Michael, 131
Overprotection, 126
Overprotective parents, 44

Parent(s), 63-66, 83-84, 93
    and school partnership, 64-66
    influence(s) of, 83-84
    pressures, 93
    relationship(s) with children, 63
Passion, 91
Peak performance, 93
Pearson, Carol, 114
Pediatrician, 43, 104
Peer group, 27, 74-76, 78-80, 88
Peewee activities, 28, 55, 61
    football, 28, 55
    sports, 61
Perfectionism, 95, 137
Personality traits, 67, 69-70
    (*see also* Temperament; Typology)

Peter Pan, 99, 114
Peter Pan syndrome, 114
Physical self-esteem, 20, 30, 46, 76-84, 103-106, 112, 124-126
    activity ,57
    aging, 103
    appearance, 20, 83-84
    attractiveness, 76, 80, 84, 103-104, 106
    attributes, 78
    beauty, 30
    changes, 77, 80, 84, 103, 112
    characteristics, 46
    development, 124
    selves, 20
    therapy, 126
Play, 53, 60, 61, 62, 94
    (*see also* Group play; solitary play)
Politics, 143
Power, 31, 72, 90, 141-142
Pre-first grade, 59
Pre-kindergarten, 59
Preadolescence, 13, 74-81
Preschool, 46, 53, 56, 59-62
    (*see also* Education; Kindergarten)
Preschool self-esteem, 56-59
    classroom, 57
    programs, 56-59
    settings, 56
    years, 62
Privileges, 132
Prostitutes, 133
Psychological orphans, 78-79
Puella, 99-100, 112
Puer, 99-100, 112, 114
Puer Aeternus, 99
Purchasing love, 38
    (*see also* Love)

Purpose, 110-111, 142-143
    (*see also* Meaning)

Quality of mood, 43
    (*see also* Temperament)

Reading, 48, 54-56, 58, 62, 130
Reading disability, 60
Recreational outlets, 123
    (*see also* Play)
Rehearsing, 96
Rejection, 75-76, 85, 87, 95, 109
Relationship(s), 21-22, 27, 46, 61, 76, 80, 85, 96, 106, 109, 117-118
Religion(s), 78
Rhythmicity, 42
    (*see also* Temperament)
Road signs, 130, 141
Roadmap, 15
Rose, X., 124
Rosenthal, Robert, 73

Schaffer, Rudolph, 40
School, 66, 136
    play, 136
    work, 66
Self-concept, 19-20
Self-confidence, 19-20
Self-esteem development, 19-143
    and cultural diversity, 135-136
    and decisions, 139-141
    and environments, 37
    and experiences, 35
    and institutions, 34-35
    and measurement, 25
    and others, 33-34
    and personalities, 35
    and social class, 37
    and the disabled, 125-131

Self-esteem development (cont.)
  and the group, 132-138
  and the influence of culture, 37-38
  and the influence of history, 36
  and women, 136-137
  as a mirror, 22
  as a spiral, 13, 21-22, 133, 137
  as developmental, 21
  definition/description, 19-38
  general, 23
  in adolescence, 82-90
  in early adulthood, 90-97
  in early childhood, 52-63
  in infants and toddlers, 39-51
  in later adulthood, 115-124
  in middle adulthood, 98-114
  in middle childhood, 64-73
  in preadolescence, 74-81
  its source, 33-38
  requirements for, 27-33
  specific, 23-24
Self-hatred, 78-80
Self-image, 19-20
Self-regard, 20
  (*see also* Self-esteem)
Self-worth, 20
  (*see also* Self-esteem)
Seligman, M. E., 41
Senex, 99-100
Senior adults, 115, 117, 122
  (*see also* Later adulthood)
Sense of purpose, 27
Separation anxiety, 89, 46, 47, 50
Sex, 92, 108
Shadow, 108-109, 113, 133
  (*see also* Dark side)
Shaffer, David, 40, 46
Shame, 44, 50, 131
Siegel, Bernie, 96

Social issues, 37, 78, 83, 126
  class 37, 83
  concern, 78
  involvement, 126
Society, 23, 44, 72, 90, 115, 118, 120, 127
Socioeconomic status, 93
Solitary play, 60
  (*see also* Group play; Play)
Soviet Union, 133
Specific attachment stage, 40
  (*see also* Attachment)
Speech, 53, 96
Spiritual issues, 118, 122
  development, 118
  life, 118, 122
Spontaneous, unstructured play, 55
  (*see also* Group play; Play; Solitary play)
Spouse, 31, 38, 93, 96, 104, 106,m 110, 120
Sternberg, Robert, 91
Sternberg's triangular theory of love, 91
  (*see also* Love)
Stone, Merlin, 138
Stranger anxiety, 46-47, 50
Stress 64, 66-68, 72
Strommen, Merton, 78
Stubbornness, 92
Success, 94, 99
Suggestions for developing self-esteem, 49, 62, 71, 79, 88-89, 96, 112, 120-122, 136-137, 139-141
  decisions to make, 139-141
  in adolescence, 88-89
  in early adulthood, 96
  in early childhood, 62
  in infants and toddlers, 49
  in later adulthood, 120-122

in middle adulthood, 112
in middle childhood, 71
in preadolescence, 79
in the disabled, 128-130
in women, 137
within subcultures, 136
within the broad culture, 134-135
Support group, 119, 134
Synchronicity, 48-49

Temperament, 39, 41-43, 49
Temporary setbacks, 88
Testing, 56, 59, 62
    (*see also* Education)
The asocial stage, 40
    (*see also* Attachment)
Thinkers, 70
    (*see also* Typology)
Thinking abilities, 83-84
Thomas Alexander, 42
Threshold of responsiveness, 43
    (*see also* Temperament)
Toddlerhood/toddlers, 39-51
    (*see also* Infancy)
True friendships, 70
Trust, 39, 44-45, 92

Trust versus mistrust, 44
Typology, 69

Unconditional love, 109
United States, 48, 92, 104, 132,
    134-135

Value issues, 78, 140
    judgments, 140
    system, 78
Violence, 92
Visual-spatial, 69
    (*see also* Intelligences)
Vocational choice(s), 86-88
Volunteer work, 110, 112, 119, 134
Von-Franz, Mary Louise, 99

Well-rounded life, 94
Wickes, Frances, 63
Wisdom, 142-143
Withdrawal, 119, 122
Women, 136-137
Work, 93-94, 139
    (*see also* Careers)
Worksheets, 56-56, 62
    (*see also* Education)

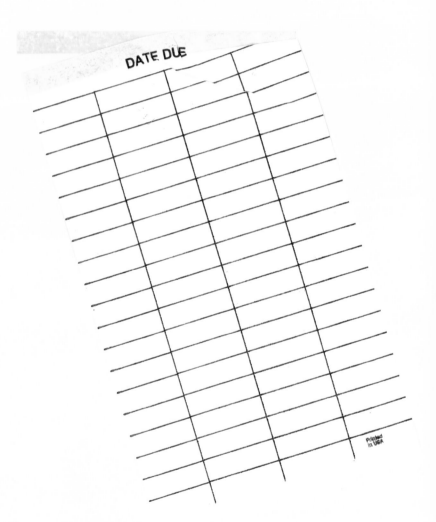

DATE DUE

Printed
in USA